SRA Open Court Reading

Skills Practice

Grade I

Mc
Graw
Hill
Education

MHEonline.com

Send all inquiries to:
McGraw-Hill Education
8787 Orion Place
Columbus, OH 43240

ISBN: 978-0-07-669288-0
MHID: 0-07-669288-4

Printed in the United States of America.

4 5 6 7 8 9 LOV 21 20 19

Table of Contents

Getting Started

Day 1 Writing Letters: Aa, Bb 1

Day 2 Writing Letters: Cc, Dd 2

Day 3 Writing Letters: Ee, Ff, Gg 3

Day 4 Writing Letters: Hh, Ii, Jj 4

Day 5 Writing Letters: Kk, Ll, Mm 5

Day 6 Writing Letters: Nn, Oo, Pp 6

Day 7 Writing Letters: Qq, Rr, Ss 7

Day 8 Writing Letters: Tt, Uu, Vv 8

Day 9 Writing Letters:
Ww, Xx, Yy, Zz 9–10

Day 10 Writing Letters:
Review A–Z .11–12

Unit 1

Lesson 1, Day 1 Phonics:
/s/ spelled s 13–14

Lesson 1, Days 1–5 Writing:
Writing about Me 15–16

Lesson 1, Day 2 Phonics:
/m/ spelled m 17–18

Lesson 1, Day 3 Phonics:
/a/ spelled a .19–20

Lesson 1, Day 4 Phonics:
/t/ spelled t and tt 21–22

**Lesson 1, Day 4 Grammar,
Usage, and Mechanics:**
Letters, Words, and Sentences 23–24

Lesson 1, Day 5 Phonics:
Review 25–26

Lesson 2, Day 1 Phonics:
/d/ spelled d 27–28

Lesson 2, Days 1–5 Writing:
Writing an Autobiography 29–30

Lesson 2, Day 2 Phonics:
/n/ spelled n 31–32

Lesson 2, Day 3 Phonics:
/i/ spelled I 33–34

Lesson 2, Day 4 Phonics:
/h/ spelled h 35–36

**Lesson 2, Day 4 Grammar,
Usage, and Mechanics:** Nouns 37–38

Lesson 2, Day 5 Phonics: Review . .39–40

Lesson 3, Day 1 Phonics:
/p/ spelled p 41–42

Lesson 3, Days 1–5 Writing:
Writing an Autobiography 43–44

Lesson 3, Day 2 Phonics:
/l/ spelled l and ll 45–46

Lesson 3, Day 3 Phonics:
/o/ spelled o 47–48

Lesson 3, Day 4 Phonics:
/b/ spelled b 49–50

**Lesson 3, Day 4 Grammar,
Usage, and Mechanics:**
Singular and Plural Nouns 51–52

Lesson 3, Day 5 Phonics:
Review 53–54

Unit 2

Lesson 1, Day 1 Phonics:
/k/ spelled c 55–56

Lesson 1, Days 1–5 Writing:
Narrative: Describe an Event 57–58

Lesson 1, Day 2 Phonics:
Special spellings al and all 59–60

Lesson 1, Day 3 Phonics:
/k/ spelled k and ■ck 61–62

Lesson 1, Day 4 Phonics:
/r/ spelled r .63–64

Lesson 1, Day 4 Grammar, Usage, and Mechanics: Adjectives **65–66**

Lesson 1, Day 5 Phonics: Review **67–68**

Lesson 2, Day 1 Phonics: /f/ spelled f and ff **69–70**

Lesson 2, Days 1–5 Writing: Narrative: Describe What Happened at School **71–72**

Lesson 2, Day 2 Phonics: /s/ spelled ss **73–74**

Lesson 2, Day 3 Phonics: /g/ spelled g **75–76**

Lesson 2, Day 4 Phonics: /j/ spelled j **77–78**

Lesson 2, Day 4 Grammar, Usage, and Mechanics: Possessive Nouns . . . **79–80**

Lesson 2, Day 5 Phonics: Review **81–82**

Lesson 3, Day 1 Phonics: /j/ spelled ▇dge **83–84**

Lesson 3, Days 1–5 Writing: Narrative: Describe What Happened at School **85–86**

Lesson 3, Day 2 Phonics: /u/ spelled u **87–88**

Lesson 3, Day 3 Phonics: /z/ spelled z and zz **89–90**

Lesson 3, Day 4 Phonics: /z/ spelled _s **91–92**

Lesson 3, Day 4 Grammar, Usage, and Mechanics: Verbs **93–94**

Lesson 3, Day 5 Phonics: Review **95–96**

Unit 3

Lesson 1, Day 1 Phonics: /ks/ spelled ▇x **97–98**

Lesson 1, Days 1–5 Writing: Informative: Describe an Object **99–100**

Lesson 1, Day 2 Phonics: /e/ spelled e **101–102**

Lesson 1, Day 3 Phonics: -ed inflectional ending (/ed/, /d/) **103–104**

Lesson 1, Day 4 Phonics: -ed inflectional ending (/t/) **105–106**

Lesson 1, Day 4 Grammar, Usage, and Mechanics: Subject / Verb Agreement **107–108**

Lesson 1, Day 5 Phonics: Review **109–110**

Lesson 2, Day 1 Phonics: /e/ spelled _ea_ **111–112**

Lesson 2, Days 1–5 Writing: Informative: Describe an Animal **113–114**

Lesson 2, Day 2 Phonics: /sh/ spelled sh **115–116**

Lesson 2, Day 3 Phonics: /th/ spelled th **117–118**

Lesson 2, Day 4 Phonics: /ch/ spelled ch **119–120**

Lesson 2, Day 4 Grammar, Usage, and Mechanics: Telling Sentences **121–122**

Lesson 2, Day 5 Phonics: Review **123–124**

Lesson 3, Day 1 Phonics: /or/ spelled or **125–126**

Lesson 3, Days 1–5 Writing: Informative: Describe a Person **127–128**

Lesson 3, Day 2 Phonics: /ar/ spelled ar **129–130**

Lesson 3, Day 3 Phonics: /w/ spelled w_ **131–132**

Lesson 3, Day 4 Phonics: /w/ spelled wh_ **133–134**

Lesson 3, Day 4 Grammar, Usage, and Mechanics: Forming Questions **135–136**

Lesson 3, Day 5 Phonics: Review **137–138**

Copyright © McGraw-Hill Education

Unit 4

Lesson 1, Day 1 Phonics:
/er/ spelled er and ir 139–140

Lesson 1, Days 1–5 Writing: Informative:
Describe a Person 141–142

Lesson 1, Day 2 Phonics:
/er/ spelled ur 143–144

Lesson 1, Day 3 Phonics:
/er/ spelled ear 145–146

Lesson 1, Day 4 Phonics:
/ng/ spelled ■ng 147–148

Lesson 1, Day 4 Grammar, Usage, and Mechanics:
Exclamatory Sentences 149–150

Lesson 1, Day 5 Phonics:
Review 151–152

Lesson 2, Day 1 Phonics:
Schwa 153–154

Lesson 2, Days 1–5 Writing:
Writing Instructions 155–156

Lesson 2, Day 2 Phonics:
Schwa -le, -el, -il, -al 157–158

Lesson 2, Day 3 Phonics:
/nk/ spelled nk 159–160

Lesson 2, Day 4 Phonics:
/kw/ spelled qu_ 161–162

Lesson 2, Day 4 Grammar, Usage, and Mechanics:
Imperative Sentences 163–164

Lesson 2, Day 5 Phonics:
Review 165–166

Lesson 3, Day 1 Phonics:
/y/ spelled y_ 167–168

Lesson 3, Days 1–5 Writing:
Writing Instructions 169–170

Lesson 3, Day 2 Phonics:
/v/ spelled v 171–172

Lesson 3, Day 3 Phonics:
/ā/ spelled a and a_e 173–174

Lesson 3, Day 4 Phonics:
Review /ā/ spelled a and a_e 175–176

Lesson 3, Day 4 Grammar, Usage, and Mechanics:
Determiners .177–178

Lesson 3, Day 5 Phonics:
Review 179–180

Unit 5

Lesson 1, Day 1 Phonics:
/ī/ spelled i and i_e 181–182

Lesson 1, Days 1–5 Writing:
Opinion Statement 183–184

Lesson 1, Day 2 Phonics:
Review /ī/ spelled i and i_e 185–186

Lesson 1, Day 3 Phonics:
/s/ spelled ce and ci_ 187–188

Lesson 1, Day 4 Phonics:
/j/ spelled ge and gi_ 189–190

Lesson 1, Day 4 Grammar, Usage, and Mechanics: Capitalization 191–192

Lesson 1, Day 5 Phonics:
Review 193–194

Lesson 2, Day 1 Phonics:
/ō/ spelled o and o_e 195–196

Lesson 2, Days 1–5 Writing:
Persuasive Poster 197–198

Lesson 2, Day 2 Phonics:
Review /ō/ spelled o and o_e 199–200

Lesson 2, Day 3 Phonics:
/ū/ spelled u and u_e 201–202

Lesson 2, Day 4 Phonics:
Review /ū/ spelled u and u_e 203–204

Lesson 2, Day 4 Grammar, Usage, and Mechanics:
Capitalization and Commas 205–206

Lesson 2, Day 5 Phonics:
Review 207–208

Lesson 3, Day 1 Phonics:
/ē/ spelled e and e_e 209–210

Lesson 3, Days 1–5 Writing:
Persuasive Poster 211–212

Lesson 3, Day 2 Phonics:
Review /ē/ spelled e and e_e 213–214

Lesson 3, Day 3 Phonics:
/ē/ spelled ee 215–216

Lesson 3, Day 4 Phonics:
/ē/ spelled ea 217–218

**Lesson 3, Day 4 Grammar,
Usage, and Mechanics:**
Using Commas and Plural Nouns 219–220

Lesson 3, Day 5 Phonics:
Review 221–222

Unit 6

Lesson 1, Day 1 Phonics:
/ē/ spelled _y 223–224

Lesson 1, Days 1–5 Writing:
Responding to Literature 225–226

Lesson 1, Day 2 Phonics:
/ē/ spelled _ie_ 227–228

Lesson 1, Day 3 Phonics:
/ē/ spelled _ey 229–230

Lesson 1, Day 4 Phonics:
Review /ē/ spelled _y, _ie_, and _ey 231–232

**Lesson 1, Day 4 Grammar, Usage,
and Mechanics:** Simple Sentences
and Subject–Verb Agreement 233–234

Lesson 1, Day 5 Phonics:
Review all /ē/ spellings 235–236

Lesson 2, Day 1 Phonics:
/s/ spelled cy 237–238

Lesson 2, Days 1–5 Writing:
Writing a Summary 239–240

Lesson 2, Day 2 Phonics:
Review /s/ spellings 241–242

Lesson 2, Day 3 Phonics:
/ā/ spelled ai_ 243–244

Lesson 2, Day 4 Phonics:
/ā/ spelled _ay 245–246

**Lesson 2, Day 4 Grammar,
Usage, and Mechanics:**
Writing Sentences 247–248

Lesson 2, Day 5 Phonics:
Review 249–250

Lesson 3, Day 1 Phonics:
/ī/ spelled _igh 251–252

Lesson 3, Days 1–5 Writing:
Responding to Literature 253–254

Lesson 3, Day 2 Phonics:
/ī/ spelled _y 255–256

Lesson 3, Day 3 Phonics:
/ī/ spelled _ie 257–258

Lesson 3, Day 4 Phonics:
Review /ī/ spelled _igh, _y, and _ie 259–260

**Lesson 3, Day 4 Grammar, Usage,
and Mechanics:** Adverbs 261–262

Lesson 3, Day 5 Phonics:
Review all /ī/ spellings 263–264

Name _____ **Date** _____

Writing Letters

A

a

B

b

Directions: Write as many letters as will fit on each line of the practice page.

Writing Letters

C

c

D

d

Directions: Write as many letters as will fit on each line of the practice page.

Writing Letters • *Skills Practice 1*

Writing Letters

Directions: Write as many letters as will fit on each line of the practice page.

Writing Letters

H

h

I

i

J

j

Directions: Write as many letters as will fit on each line of the practice page.

Writing Letters

Directions: Write as many letters as will fit on each line of the practice page.

Writing Letters

N _____

n _____

O _____

o _____

P _____

p _____

Directions: Write as many letters as will fit on each line of the practice page.

Writing Letters

Q

q

R

r

S

s

Directions: Write as many letters as will fit on each line of the practice page.

Writing Letters

Directions: Write as many letters as will fit on each line of the practice page.

Writing Letters

Directions: Write as many letters as will fit on each line of the practice page.

Writing Letters

Y

y

Z

z

Directions: Write as many letters as will fit on each line of the practice page.

Writing Letters • *Skills Practice 1*

Lowercase Letters

Directions: Connect the dots from a to z.

Capital Letters

Directions: Connect the dots from A to Z.

Sounds and Spellings

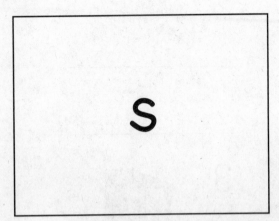

S

s _ _ _ _ _ _ _ _ _   S _ _ _ _ _ _ _ _

Practice

Directions: Practice writing s and S. At the bottom write s on the line near each picture that begins with the /s/ sound.

Apply

1.

   _____

   - - - - - - - - -

   _____

2.

   _____

   - - - - - - - - -

   _____

3.

   _____

   - - - - - - - - -

   _____

4.

   _____

   - - - - - - - - -

   _____

5.

   _____

   - - - - - - - - -

   _____

6.

   _____

   - - - - - - - - -

   _____

7.

   _____

   - - - - - - - - -

   _____

8.

   _____

   - - - - - - - - -

   _____

Directions: Name the pictures. Write the letter s under the picture if it begins or ends with the /s/ sound.

Writing about Me

Think

Create a drawing of yourself.

Prewriting

Brainstorm a list of words about your picture.

1. _____

2. _____

3. _____

4. _____

Revising
Use this checklist to make your writing better.

☐ Did your drawing help you think of writing ideas?

☐ Did you include all the information from your brainstorming list in your sentence?

☐ Did you add words to give more detail to your writing?

Editing
Use this checklist to help you correct mistakes in your writing.

☐ Are your letters spaced correctly?

☐ Are you writing from left to right and top to bottom?

Publishing
Use this checklist to get your writing ready to share.

☐ Draw your picture on a clean sheet of paper.

☐ Copy your sentence neatly below your drawing.

☐ Display your work in the classroom.

Sounds and Spellings

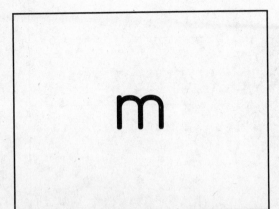

Practice

Directions: Practice writing *m* and *M*. Name each picture and write the letter *m* on the line under each picture that begins with the /m/ sound.

Skills Practice 1 • Phonics

Apply

1.
_____ _____
- - - - - - - - - - - - - -
_____ _____

2.
_____ _____
- - - - - - - - - - - - - -
_____ _____

3.
_____ _____
- - - - - - - - - - - - - -
_____ _____

4.
_____ _____
- - - - - - - - - - - - - -
_____ _____

5.
_____ _____
- - - - - - - - - - - - - -
_____ _____

6.
_____ _____
- - - - - - - - - - - - - -
_____ _____

7.
_____ _____
- - - - - - - - - - - - - -
_____ _____

8.
_____ _____
- - - - - - - - - - - - - -
_____ _____

Directions: Write the letter *m* in the first space if you hear the /m/ sound at the beginning of the word. Write the letter *m* in the second space if you hear the /m/ sound at the end of the word.

Phonics • *Skills Practice 1*

Sounds and Spellings

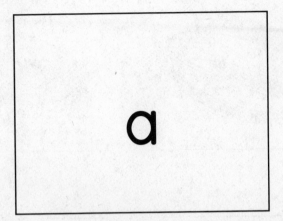

Practice

a   A

1. Sam is in a b nd .

2. Jack used a m p .

Directions: Practice writing a and A. Listen as the teacher reads each sentence.
Write the missing letter to complete the word.

Skills Practice 1 • Phonics   UNIT 1 • Lesson 1 • Day 3 **19**

Apply

3.

_____

- - - - - - - - - - - - - - -

_____

4.

_____

- - - - - - - - - - - - - - -

_____

5.

_____

- - - - - - - - - - - - - - -

_____

6.

_____

- - - - - - - - - - - - - - -

_____

7.

_____

- - - - - - - - - - - - - - -

_____

8.

_____

- - - - - - - - - - - - - - -

_____

9.

_____

- - - - - - - - - - - - - - -

_____

10.

_____

- - - - - - - - - - - - - - -

_____

11.

_____

- - - - - - - - - - - - - - -

_____

Directions: Name each picture. Write a on the line if you hear the /a/ sound in the word.

Phonics • *Skills Practice 1*

Sounds and Spellings

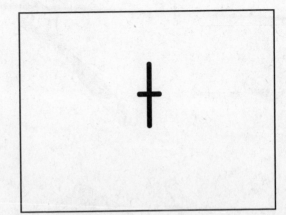

Practice

 — — — — — —  — — — — —

_____   _____   _____

— — — — — — —   — — — — — — —   — — — — — — —

_____   _____   _____

Directions: Practice writing *t* and *T*. Write the letter *t* if you hear the /t/ sound at the beginning of the word.

Apply

1.

2.

3.

4.

Directions: Name each picture. Write the letter *t* on the left side of the picture if the picture begins with the /t/ sound. Write the letter *t* on the right of the picture if the picture ends with the /t/ sound.

Phonics • *Skills Practice 1*

Letters, Words, and Sentences
Focus

Rule	Example
• **Letters** make **words**.	h a t hat
• Words make **sentences**.	I can fly a kite.

Practice

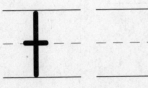
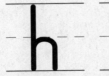

t   h   e

the

I see Sam.

_____

- - - - - - - - - - - - - - - - -

_____

I can see.

_____

- - - - - - - - - - - - - - - - -

_____

Directions: Listen to the letters, word, and sentence. Write them in the spaces provided.

Apply

1. cow

_____

- - - - - - - - - - - - - -

_____

2. cat

_____

- - - - - - - - - - - - - -

_____

3. dog

_____

- - - - - - - - - - - - - -

_____

4. bug

_____

- - - - - - - - - - - - - -

_____

5. bat

_____

- - - - - - - - - - - - - -

_____

Directions: Listen to each word. Repeat the word. Then, draw a line from the word to the correct picture, and copy the word on the line next to its picture.

Sounds and Spellings Review

1. The cat sat.

   The cat is on the hat.

_____

– –

_____

2. Matt has a hat.

   Matt has a ham.

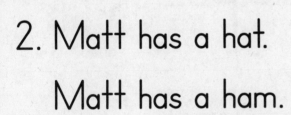

_____

– –

_____

Directions: Listen as the teacher reads each sentence. Choose the sentence that matches
the picture and write that sentence on the line.

Sounds and Spellings Review

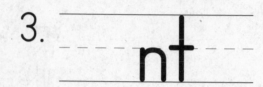

3. ___nt

4. ___un

5. ___ap

6. ___ent

Directions: Write the letter that makes the sound you hear at the beginning of each picture to spell a word.

Phonics • *Skills Practice 1*

Sounds and Spellings

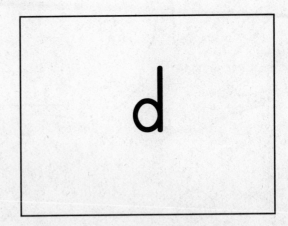

Practice

d

D

Dad _____    mad _____

1. Dad was sad.

_____

Directions: Practice writing *d* and *D*. Write the words and sentence.

Apply

2.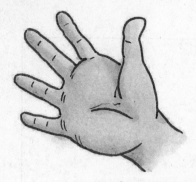

　　———————————　　———————————
　　- - - - - - - -　　- - - - - - - -
　　———————————　　———————————

3.

　　———————————　　———————————
　　- - - - - - - -　　- - - - - - - -
　　———————————　　———————————

4.

　　———————————　　———————————
　　- - - - - - - -　　- - - - - - - -
　　———————————　　———————————

5.

　　———————————　　———————————
　　- - - - - - - -　　- - - - - - - -
　　———————————　　———————————

Directions: Write the letter *d* on the first line if you hear /d/ at the beginning of the word. Write the letter *d* on the second line if you hear /d/ at the end of the word.

Phonics • *Skills Practice 1*

Writing an Autobiography
Think

Audience: Who will read your autobiography?

_____

- -

_____

- -

_____

Purpose: What is your reason for writing an autobiography?

_____

- -

_____

- -

_____

Prewriting
Create a list below to help organize your ideas.

1. _____

2. _____

3. _____

4. _____

5. _____

Sounds and Spellings

Practice

n N

Directions: Practice writing *n* and *N*. Write the letter *n* if the picture begins with the /n/ sound.

Apply

1.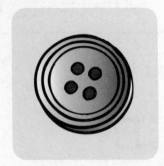

_____   _____

- - - - - - -   - - - - - - -

_____   _____

2.

_____   _____

- - - - - - -   - - - - - - -

_____   _____

3.

_____   _____

- - - - - - -   - - - - - - -

_____   _____

4.

_____   _____

- - - - - - -   - - - - - - -

_____   _____

Directions: Write the letter *n* on the first line if you hear /n/ at the beginning of the word. Write the letter *n* on the second line if you hear /n/ at the end of the word.

Phonics • *Skills Practice 1*

Sounds and Spellings

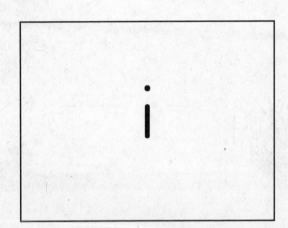

Practice

1.

2.

3.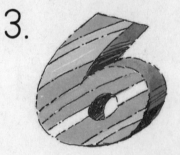

_____ _____ _____

Directions: Practice writing *i* and *I*. Name the pictures.
Write *i* if you hear /i/ in the word.

Apply

4. _____

5.

_____

6.

_____

7.

_____

8.

_____

Directions: Write the word *mitt* beside Tim's baseball mitt at the top of the page. Name each picture. Write *i* if you hear /i/ in the word.

Phonics • *Skills Practice 1*

Sounds and Spellings

h_

Practice

h_
H_

hat   ham   hand

_____   _____   _____

Directions: Practice writing h_ and H_. Write the words that
begin with the /h/ sound.

Apply

1.

_____
- - - - - - - - -
_____

2.

_____
- - - - - - - - -
_____

3.

_____
- - - - - - - - -
_____

4.

_____
- - - - - - - - -
_____

5.

_____
- - - - - - - - -
_____

6.

_____
- - - - - - - - -
_____

Dictation

_____
- - - - - - - - -
_____

Directions: Write the letter _h_ if the picture begins with the /h/ sound.

36 UNIT 1 • Lesson 2 • Day 4

Phonics • *Skills Practice 1*

Nouns
Focus

Rule	Examples
Nouns are words that name a person, place, or thing.	Sid mill sand

Practice

jump

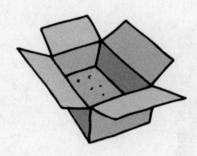

open

Post Office

nurse

Directions: Listen to the name of each picture. Draw a circle around the picture if the word is a noun.

Apply

1.

2.

3.

4.

5.

Directions: Listen to the name of each noun. Decide if it is a person, place, or thing.
Draw an x through the nouns that name a person, a circle around those that name a
place, and a line through the nouns that name a thing.

Sounds and Spellings Review

i	h	d	n

1.

_____

- - - - -

_____am

2.

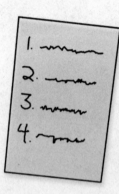

_____

l - - - - st

3.

_____

- - - - -

pa_____

4.

_____ _____

- - - - - - - -

_____an_____

Directions: Name each picture, and fill in the missing letter in the space provided to spell each word. You will use some letters more than once.

Sounds and Spellings Review

d n i h a s m t

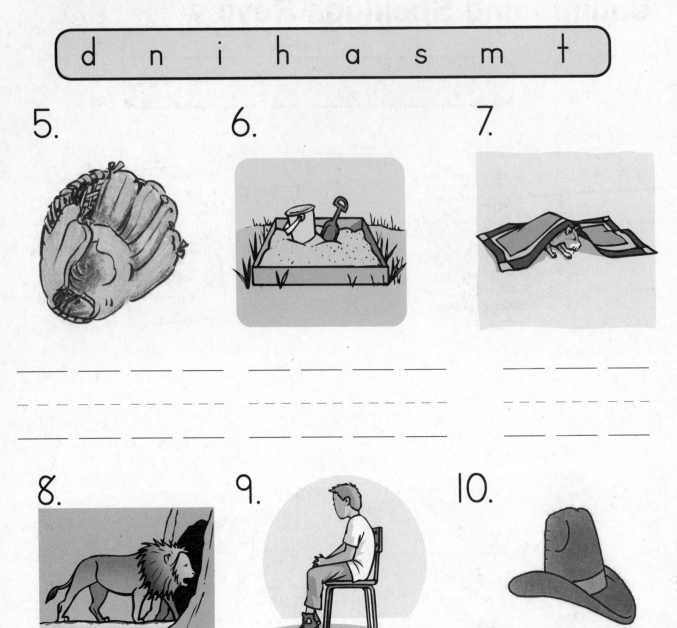

5.

6.

7.

8.

9.

10.

Directions: Name the picture. Say the sounds and write the word on the line. Use the letters in the box to help you.

Phonics • *Skills Practice 1*

Sounds and Spellings

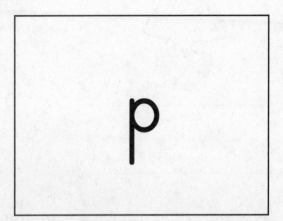

Practice

Directions: Practice writing *p* and *P*. Circle the six objects in the picture that begin with the /p/ sound.

Apply

1.

_____

- - - - - - - -

_____

2.

_____

- - - - - - - -

_____

3.

_____

- - - - - - - -

_____

4.

_____

- - - - - - - -

_____

Dictation

_____

- - - - - - - - - - - - - - - - - - -

_____

_____

- - - - - - - - - - - - - - - - - - -

_____

Directions: Name the pictures. Write the letter *p* if the picture begins or ends with the /p/ sound.

Phonics • *Skills Practice 1*

Revising

Use this checklist to make your autobiography better.

☐ Did you draw pictures to help you think of writing ideas?

☐ Did you include all the information from your list?

☐ Did you add words to give more detail to your writing?

Editing

Use this checklist to help you correct mistakes in your autobiography.

☐ Are your letters and words spaced correctly?

☐ Have you used singular and plural nouns correctly?

Publishing
Use this checklist to get your autobiography ready to share.

☐ Copy your autobiography on a clean sheet of paper.

☐ Create a cover for your writing.

Sounds and Spellings

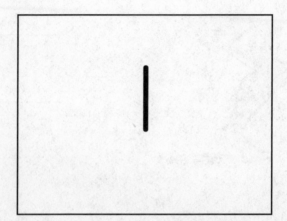

Practice

I L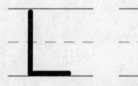

1.

_____

- - - - - - - - - - - - - -

_____

2.

_____

- - - - - - - - - - - - - -

_____

3.

_____

- - - - - - - - - - - - - -

_____

4.

_____

- - - - - - - - - - - - - -

_____

Directions: Practice writing l and L. Name each picture. Write the letter l if you hear /l/ at the beginning of the word.

Apply

5. 
_____   _____
- - - - - - - -   - - - - - - - -
_____   _____

6. 
_____   _____
- - - - - - - -   - - - - - - - -
_____   _____

7. 
_____   _____
- - - - - - - -   - - - - - - - -
_____   _____

8. 
_____   _____
- - - - - - - -   - - - - - - - -
_____   _____

Directions: Write *l* on the first line if you hear the /l/ sound at the beginning of the word. Write *l* on the second line if you hear the /l/ sound at the end of the word.

Phonics • *Skills Practice 1*

Sounds and Spellings

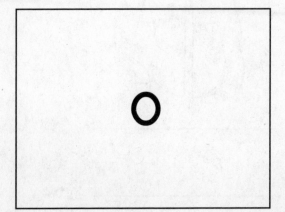

Practice

O

O

Directions: Practice writing o and O. Write o on the line if you hear the /o/ sound in the word that names the picture.

Apply

1.

_____

- - - - - - - - - - -

_____

2.

_____

- - - - - - - - - - -

_____

3.

_____

- - - - - - - - - - -

_____

4.

_____

- - - - - - - - - - -

_____

Dictation

_____   _____

- - - - - - - - - -   - - - - - - - - - -

_____   _____

_____   _____

- - - - - - - - - -   - - - - - - - - - -

_____   _____

Directions: Name each picture. Write o if you hear the /o/ sound in the word.

Sounds and Spellings

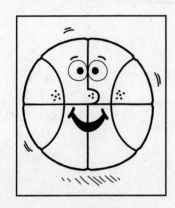

b

Practice

b ———————— B ————

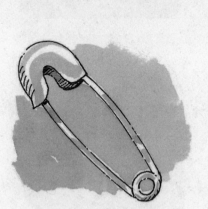

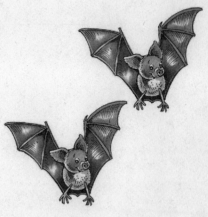

hat   bat   pan   pin   bats   sad

Directions: Practice writing *b* and *B*. Circle the word that names the picture.

Apply

1.

_____

- - - - - - - - - - -

_____

2.

_____

- - - - - - - - - - -

_____

3.

_____

- - - - - - - - - - -

_____

4.

_____

- - - - - - - - - - -

_____

Directions: Name the pictures. Write the letter *b* on the line before the picture if the picture begins with the /b/ sound. Write the letter *b* on the line after the picture if the picture ends with the /b/ sound.

Singular and Plural Nouns
Focus

Rule	Example
Add **s** to a noun to show that there is more than one.	hat hat**s**

Practice

1.   flag   flags

2.   pig   pigs

3.   swing   swings

4.   flower   flowers

Directions: Listen to the name of each picture. Circle the word that shows if the picture is one or more than one.

Apply

5. pig

_____

- - - - - - - - - - - - - - -

_____

6. cow

_____

- - - - - - - - - - - - - - -

_____

7. carrot

_____

- - - - - - - - - - - - - - -

_____

8. boat

_____

- - - - - - - - - - - - - - -

_____

Directions: Listen to the name of each picture. Copy the word on the line. Then, change the word so it means more than one.

Grammar, Usage, and Mechanics • *Skills Practice 1*

Sounds and Spellings Review

s	t	m	i	a	p	o	l

1.

—— —— —— ——

2.

—— —— —— ——

3.

—— —— —— ——

Directions: Name the picture. Say the sounds and write the word on the line. Use the letters in the box to help you.

Sounds and Spellings Review

4. Dan has a _____ .

band
bat

5. The doll is not _____ .

pad
sad

Dictation

_____   _____

_____   _____

_____   _____

Directions: Look at the picture. Write the word that completes
the sentence.

Sounds and Spellings

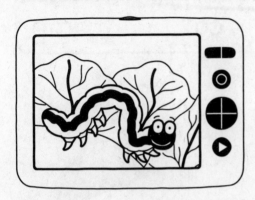

C

c

C

Practice

 _____

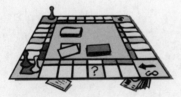 _____

 _____

 _____

Directions: Practice writing c and C. Write c next to each picture whose name begins with the /k/ sound.

Apply

can	clap	cot	cat	camp

1.

_____

_____

2.

_____

_____

3.

_____

_____

4.

_____

_____

5.

_____

_____

Dictation

_____   _____

_____   _____

_____   _____

_____   _____

Directions: Name each picture. Find the word from the word box that rhymes with it. Write the word on the line.

Narrative: Describe an Event

Think

Audience: Who will read your description?

_____

_____

Purpose: What do you want your description
to do?

_____

_____

Prewriting

**Use the Sequence Map to brainstorm
descriptive words or phrases about your topic.**

Topic:	

First	Next

Then	Last

Revising
Use this checklist to make your description better.

☐ Did you use a sequence map to help you stay organized?

☐ Did you write details on your sequence map?

☐ Do the details in your description help the reader picture the event?

Editing
Use this checklist to help make corrections to your description.

☐ Are all the words spelled correctly?

☐ Did you write in complete sentences?

☐ Do your sentences begin with capital letters and end with punctuation?

Publishing
Use this checklist to get your description ready to share.

☐ Copy your description onto a clean sheet of paper or into your Writer's Notebook.

☐ Add an illustration to your writing.

Sounds and Spellings

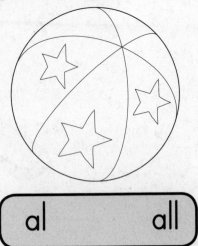

al   all

Practice

1. call

2. hall

3. bald

4. The tall man hit the ball.

Directions: Write the words and the sentence in the space provided. The spellings *al* and *all* make the /aw/ sound as in *saw*.

Apply

5.

s _____ t

6.

c _____

7.

8.

t _____   sm _____

Directions: Name each picture. Use the letters *al* or *all* to complete the words.

Sounds and Spellings

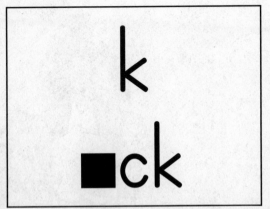

k

 k — — — — — — 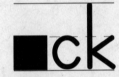 —ck — — — — — — —

K _____

Practice

1. — — — — — —

2. — — — — — —

3. — — — — — —

4. — — — — — —

Directions: Practice writing *k*, ■*ck* and *K*. Use a green crayon to draw a box next to each ■*ck* spelling. Write *k* next to each picture whose name begins with the /k/ sound.

Apply

5.
_____
- - - - - - - - -
_____

6.
_____
- - - - - - - - -
_____

7.
_____
- - - - - - - - -
_____

8.
_____
- - - - - - - - -
_____

9.
_____
- - - - - - - - -
_____

10.
_____
- - - - - - - - -
_____

Directions: Name each picture and write the word on the blank. Use the letters on the king's coins to help you.

Phonics • *Skills Practice 1*

Sounds and Spellings

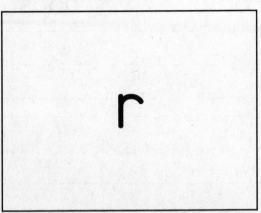

r

r

R

Practice

Directions: Practice writing r and R. Place an X on the picture if it begins with the /r/ sound.

Apply

1. ramp. A   naps   crab   on   a

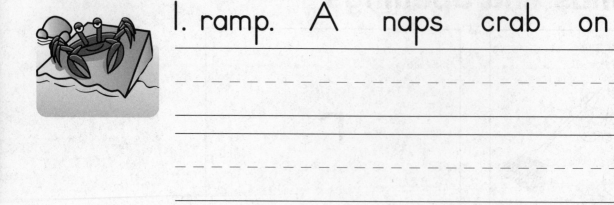

2. robin.   can   I   see   a

Dictation

Directions: Look at each picture. Unscramble the words to make a sentence that tells about the picture. Write the sentence correctly on the lines.

Adjectives
Focus

> **Rule**
> **Adjectives** are describing words that tell more about something.
>
> **Example**
> The **frisky** cat runs.

Practice

> black   crisp   tan   small

The puppy has a _____ nose

and _____ eyes.

He has _____ spots.

He has a _____ bone.

Directions: Listen to the words and sentences. Complete each sentence with the word that describes the picture.

Apply

black	sick	tall	small	hot

1. _____

2. _____

3. _____

4. _____

5. _____

Directions: Look at each picture clue. Find the best adjective in the box that describes the picture. Write it on the line.

Grammar, Usage, and Mechanics • *Skills Practice 1*

Sounds and Spellings Review

| ram | ball | crab | cat |

1.

_____

- - - - - - - - - - -

_____

2.

_____

- - - - - - - - - - -

_____

3.

_____

- - - - - - - - - - -

_____

4.

_____

- - - - - - - - - - -

_____

Directions: Read the words in the box. Write the word on the line that names each picture.

Sounds and Spellings Review

block

crack

rock

Dictation

_____

- -

_____

- -

_____

- -

_____

Directions: Read the words. Then connect each word to its picture.

Phonics • *Skills Practice 1*

Sounds and Spellings

f

Practice

1.
_____

2.
_____

3.
- - - - - - - - - -

Directions: Practice writing *f* and *F*. Then write the letter *f* on the line if the picture begins with the /f/ sound.

Apply

4. Pam has a _____.

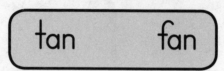

| tan | fan |

5. Did Jim see the

_____?

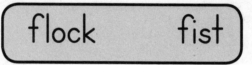

| flock | fist |

6. Kim uses her nose to

_____.

| staff | sniff |

Directions: Look at each picture. Listen as the teacher reads the sentences. Write the word from the box that correctly completes each sentence.

Phonics • *Skills Practice 1*

Narrative: Describe What Happened at School

Think

Audience: Who will read your story?

_____

_____

Purpose: What do you want your story to do?

_____

_____

Prewriting

Use the Story Map to plan your story.

Beginning

↓

Middle

↓

End

Sounds and Spellings

ss

pass _____

_____

miss _____

_____

hiss _____

Practice

Bess gives her baby brother a kiss.

_____   _____

_____   _____

Directions: Practice writing words ending in ss. Listen to the teacher read the sentence. Write the
two words that end with the ss spelling.

Apply

l   s o s f

_____

- - - - - - - - - - - - - - - - - - -

_____

o   s t s

_____

- - - - - - - - - - - - - - - - - - -

_____

Dictation

_____

- - - - - - - - - - - - - - - - - - -

_____

- - - - - - - - - - - - - - - - - - -

_____

- - - - - - - - - - - - - - - - - - -

_____

Directions: Unscramble the letters to correctly name the picture. Write the word on the line.

Sounds and Spellings

g

g

G

Practice

1. The dog can see a bag.

Directions: Practice writing g and G. Read and copy the sentence.

Skills Practice 1 • Phonics

Apply

2. The pig has a grin.
The tag has a pig.

_____

- - - - - - - - - - - - - - - - - - -

_____

3. The frog is on the golf ball.
The frog sits in the grass.

_____

- - - - - - - - - - - - - - - - - - -

_____

- - - - - - - - - - - - - - - - - - -

_____

Directions: Write the sentence that describes each picture.

Sounds and Spellings

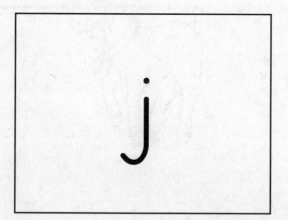

j

j

J

Practice

1. Jan can _____.

2. Jill got _____.

Directions. Practice writing *j* and *J*. Look at each picture. Read each sentence. Complete the sentence with the word that names the picture.

Apply

3.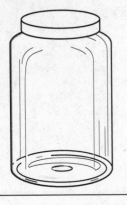

_____

- - - - - - - - -

_____

4.

_____

- - - - - - - - -

_____

5.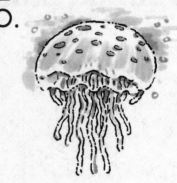

_____

- - - - - - - - -

_____

Dictation

_____

- - - - - - - - - - - - - - - - - -

_____

_____

- - - - - - - - - - - - - - - - - -

_____

_____

- - - - - - - - - - - - - - - - - -

_____

Directions: Write the letter *j* on the line if the picture begins with the /j/ sound.

Phonics • *Skills Practice 1*

Possessive Nouns
Focus

Rule	Example
Add **'s** to a common noun or proper noun to show ownership.	Frank**'s** mitt rabbit**'s** ears

Practice

ball	glass	frog	sack

1. I am not big.

   I can hop.

   I am green.

   I belong to Pam.

   I am _____

   _ _ _ _ _ _ _ _ _ _ _ _ _ .

2. Jack fills me with water.

   Jack fills me with milk.

   Jack gulps and sips from me.

   I am _____

   _ _ _ _ _ _ _ _ _ _ _ _ _

   _____ .

Directions: Listen to each riddle. Write the possessive noun and what belongs to that noun.

Apply

| cap | jacket | ball | bat | mitt | hands |

3. _____ grip the bat.

4. _____ is on the backstop.

5. _____ is cracked.

6. _____ is in the dust.

Directions: Look at the picture. Listen to each sentence. Write the possessive noun that tells
who owns something and what object belongs to that person.

Sounds and Spellings Review

| gift | dress | flag | jet |

1.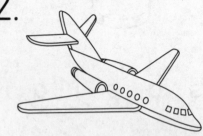

_____

_ _ _ _ _ _ _ _ _

_____

2.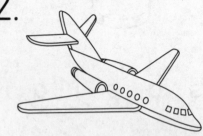

_____

_ _ _ _ _ _ _ _ _

_____

3.

_____

_ _ _ _ _ _ _ _ _

_____

4.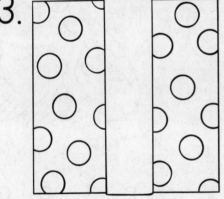

_____

_ _ _ _ _ _ _ _ _

_____

Directions: Write the word from the word box that names each picture.

Sounds and Spellings Review

5.

s a s l g

_____

- - - - - - - -

_____

6.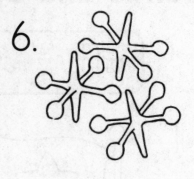

c k s j a

_____

- - - - - - - -

_____

7.

i n f

_____

- - - - - - - -

_____

8.

r f o g

_____

- - - - - - - -

_____

Directions: Unscramble the letters to correctly name the picture. Write the word on the line.

Phonics • *Skills Practice 1*

Sounds and Spellings

■dge _____

Practice

1. ridge _____

2. lodge _____

3. dodge _____

Directions: Practice writing ■*dge*. Use a green crayon to draw the box in each
dge spelling. Read and write each word.

Apply

4.

d g e i r b

_____

- - - - - - - - - -

_____

5.

d e b a g

_____

- - - - - - - - - -

_____

Dictation

_____

- -

_____

_____

- -

_____

_____

- -

_____

Directions: Unscramble the letters to correctly name the picture. Write the word on the line.

Phonics • *Skills Practice 1*

Revising
Use this checklist to make your story better.

☐ Did you use all your ideas from your story map?

☐ Does your story have a beginning, a middle, and an end?

☐ Does your story address your audience and purpose?

Editing
Use this checklist to check the narrative.

☐ Did you write a title for your story?

☐ Do all words have correct spellings?

☐ Did you write in complete sentences?

☐ Do all sentences begin with capital letters and have the correct end marks?

Publishing

Use this checklist to get the narrative ready to share.

☐ Copy your story onto a clean sheet of paper or into your Writer's Notebook.

☐ Create a picture for your story.

Sounds and Spellings

u

u

U

Practice

_____   _____

1. rug _____   2. sun _____

_____   _____

3. mug _____   4. nut _____

Directions: Practice writing u and U. Read and write the words with the /u/ sound.

Apply

5.

c u d k

_____

- - - - - - - - -

_____

6.

u s m p t

_____

- - - - - - - - -

_____

7.

m d u

_____

- - - - - - - - -

_____

8.

p c u

_____

- - - - - - - - -

_____

9.

m u d r

_____

- - - - - - - - -

_____

10.

p p u

_____

- - - - - - - - -

_____

Directions: Unscramble the letters and write the word on the line that correctly names the picture.

Phonics • *Skills Practice 1*

Sounds and Spellings

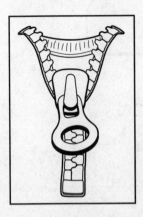

Z   ZZ

Z _____

ZZ _____

Practice

1. Did Zack see fuzz on the mat?

_____

_____

_____

Directions: Practice writing z and zz. Then copy the sentence.

Apply

buzz	jazz	zip

2.

_____

- - - - - - - - - -

_____

3.

_____

- - - - - - - - - -

_____

4.

_____

- - - - - - - - - -

_____

Dictation

_____   _____

- - - - - - - - -   - - - - - - - - -

_____   _____

- - - - - - - - -   - - - - - - - - -

_____   _____

- - - - - - - - -   - - - - - - - - -

_____   _____

Directions: Write the word that names each picture. Use the words in the box to help you.

Phonics • *Skills Practice 1*

Sounds and Spellings

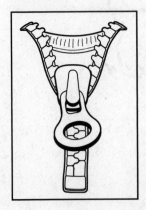

_s

_s

Practice

1. rug

2. rugs

3. pan

4. pans

Directions: Practice writing _s. Read and write each word. Circle each word that ends with /z/ spelled _s.

Apply

5.

6.

7.

8.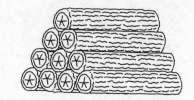

9.

10.

Directions: Place an X on the picture if it ends with the /z/ sound.

Phonics • *Skills Practice 1*

Verbs
Focus

Rule	Example
Verbs show action.	They **run** to the park. Andy **rides** his bike.

Practice

> smell   fixed   hug   sip   sit

1. Jeff and Jan _____

   Gram and Granddad.

2. Gram _____ us muffins.

3. We _____ and _____

   milk at Gram's.

Directions: Look at each picture. Listen to each sentence.
Write the word that tells the action to complete each sentence.

Apply

4. The man is petting his dog.

_____

_____

5. Tom has filled the glass.

_____

_____

6. Kim has napped in the bed.

_____

_____

7. Ben and Nan have helped a lost cat.

_____

_____

8. He was selling milk and jam.

_____

_____

Directions: Read each sentence. Circle the helping verb and underline the action verb. Then copy the verb on the line.

Sounds and Spellings Review

| suds | bugs | judge | zigzag |

1.

_____

- - - - - - - - - - - - - -

_____

2.

_____

- - - - - - - - - - - - - -

_____

3.

_____

- - - - - - - - - - - - - -

_____

4.

_____

- - - - - - - - - - - - - -

_____

Directions: Write the word from the word box that names each picture.

Skills Practice 1 • Phonics

Sounds and Spellings Review

5. The bus is on the bridge.
The bus is black.

_____

- -

_____

- -

_____

Dictation

_____   _____

- - - - - - - - - - - - - - -   - - - - - - - - - - - - - - -

_____   _____

- - - - - - - - - - - - - - -   - - - - - - - - - - - - - - -

_____   _____

- - - - - - - - - - - - - - -   - - - - - - - - - - - - - - -

_____   _____

Directions: Write the sentence that describes the picture.

Phonics • *Skills Practice 1*

Sounds and Spellings

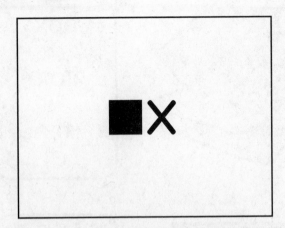

Practice

1.

2.

3.

_____

_____

Directions: Practice writing ■x and ■X in the spaces provided. Use a green crayon to draw the green box in the ■x spelling. At the bottom, name each picture. Write x if you hear the /ks/ sound at the end of the word.

Apply

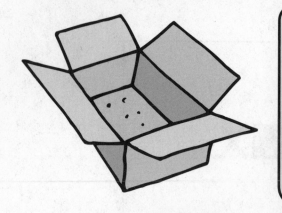

box	4.
fox	
ox	

fuzz	5.
tux	
six	

Dictation

Directions: Circle the word that names each picture. Then write the word on the line.

Phonics • *Skills Practice 1*

Informative: Describe an Object

Think

Audience: Who will read your description?

_____

_____

Purpose: What do you want your description to do?

_____

_____

Prewriting

Use the cluster web to organize descriptive words or phrases about your topic.

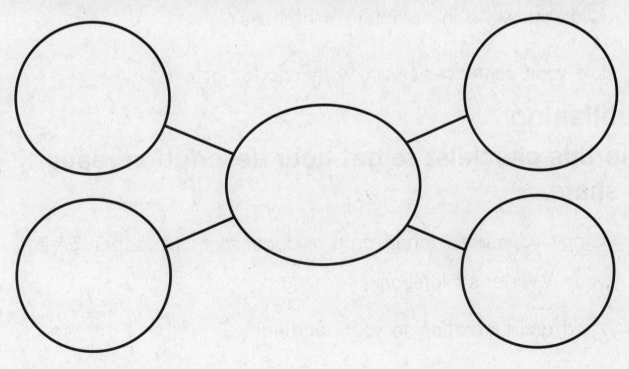

Revising
Use this checklist to make your description better.

☐ Did you use your cluster web to help you organize descriptive words for your writing?

☐ Did you write details on your web?

☐ Do the details in your description help the reader picture the object?

Editing
Use this checklist to help make corrections to your description.

☐ Are all the words spelled correctly?

☐ Did you write in complete sentences?

☐ Do your sentences begin with capital letters?

Publishing
Use this checklist to get your description ready to share.

☐ Copy your description onto a clean sheet of paper or into your Writer's Notebook.

☐ Add an illustration to your writing.

Sounds and Spellings

e

_____ e _____

_____ E _____

Practice

The _____ e _____ has a

n _____ s _____ .

Directions: Practice writing e and E. Use the picture to help you fill in the missing letters in the words in the sentence.

Apply

1.

_____

- - - - - - - - - - - -

_____

2.

_____

- - - - - - - - - - - -

_____

k d e s   s r e d s   e t m l   e d l s

3.

_____

- - - - - - - - - - - -

_____

4.

_____

- - - - - - - - - - - -

_____

Directions: Name each picture. Unscramble the letters to spell the word.
Write the word correctly on the line.

Phonics • *Skills Practice 1*

Sounds and Spellings

Rule

The inflectional ending –ed is added to a verb. It shows that the action happened in the past. The ending –ed can make several sounds.

Two of the sounds it can make are: /ed/ and /d/. If the last sound of the word is /d/ or /t/, the –ed ending will sound like /ed/.

Practice

> dusted   pinned
>
> sobbed   mended

ed

d

_____

- - - - - - - - - - - - - - - - -

_____

_____

- - - - - - - - - - - - - - - - -

_____

Directions: Read the words. Listen for the sound the letters -ed make at the end of the word. Write the word under the correct bag.

Apply

planned

dented

ed

rusted

dimmed

d

wagged

ended

Dictation

Directions: Read the words. Draw a line to match the word to the peanut with the ending sound
that the word makes.

104 UNIT 3 • Lesson 1 • Day 3

Phonics • *Skills Practice 1*

Sounds and Spellings

> **Rule**
> The inflectional ending *-ed* can also make the /t/ sound. | If the last sound of the word is /k/, /f/, /p/, or /s/, the *-ed* ending will sound like /t/.

picked _____

missed _____

helped _____

Practice

> popped   hinted   linked   begged

_____

_____

_____

Directions: Say each word and listen for the /t/ sound the letters *-ed* make at the end of the word. Write the words on the lines. Next, read the words in the box. Write the words that end with the /t/ sound on the lines.

Apply

1. Kim _____ on the rug.

   [tripped   locked]

2. Bob _____ the truck.

   [lasted   stopped]

3. The dog _____ my hand.

   [licked   passed]

4. Alex _____ his mom.

   [missed   mixed]

5. Sam _____ his dad.

   [tugged   helped]

Directions: Complete each sentence with the correct word from the box. Read the word and write the word on the line. Listen for the *t* sound at the end of each correct answer.

Subject / Verb Agreement

Focus

Rules	Examples
• Complete sentences must always have a subject and a verb. • A subject and verb must agree in a sentence. If the subject is singular, the verb must agree with it. If the subject is plural, the verb must agree with it.	The cat runs up the tree. The cats run up the tree.

Practice

1. Tim and Jill stand in the hall.

_____

- -

_____

2. Sam can see the boat.

_____

- -

_____

Directions: Listen to the sentences. Write the sentences correctly, leaving a space between the words. Use a capital letter to start each sentence. Circle the subject of the sentence (the noun) and underline the action in the sentence (the verb).

Apply

3. Kids (stand, stands) in the hall.

_____

- -

_____

4. The bird (fly, flies) in the sky.

_____

- -

_____

Directions: Listen to the sentences. Choose the correct verb to agree with the subject. Rewrite the sentences on the lines using the correct verb.

Sounds and Spellings Review

ed   d   t

locked   listed

buzzed   pinned

camped   spotted

sanded   pressed

Directions: Read the word on each crayon. Listen for the sound the ending -ed makes at the end of the word. Color the crayon brown if you hear /ed/. Color the crayon blue if you hear /d/. Color the crayon green if you hear /t/.

Sounds and Spellings Review

best	spell	mix

1.

2.

3.

Dictation

Directions: Name each picture. Write the word that rhymes with it on the line under the picture.

Sounds and Spellings

_ea_

Practice

| breakfast | treadmill | headband | bread |

_____

Ben has a _____. He ran on

the _____. He can have

_____.

He has

_____ and jam.

Directions: Look at the picture. Complete each sentence with a word from the word box. Write the words on the lines.

Apply

spread   lead   read   headset   bread

1.

_____

- - - - - - - - - - -

_____

2.

_____

- - - - - - - - - - -

_____

3.

_____

- - - - - - - - - - -

_____

4.

_____

- - - - - - - - - - -

_____

5.

_____

- - - - - - - - - - -

_____

Directions: Write the word that names each picture.

Informative: Describe an Animal
Think
Audience: Who will read your description?

_____

_____

Purpose: What do you want your description to do?

_____

_____

Prewriting
Brainstorm a list of animals you can describe.

1. _____

2. _____

3. _____

4. _____

Revising
Use this checklist to make your description better.

☐ Did you use ideas from your brainstorming list?

☐ Did you choose one animal to write about?

☐ Do the details in your description help the readers clearly picture that animal?

Editing
Use this checklist to help you check your description.

☐ Did you write a title for your story?

☐ Are all words spelled correctly?

☐ Did you write in complete sentences?

☐ Did you use adjectives in your writing?

Publishing
Use this checklist to get the narrative ready to share.

☐ Copy your story onto a clean sheet of paper.

☐ Add an illustration that matches your description.

Sounds and Spellings

sh

sh

Practice

Directions: Practice writing *sh* in the space provided. At the bottom, name each picture.
Write *sh* if you hear the /sh/ sound in the word.

Apply

1.

s h r t a

_____

- - - - - - - - -

_____

2.

r s b u h

_____

- - - - - - - - -

_____

3.

l e l s h

_____

- - - - - - - - -

_____

4.

a h c s

_____

- - - - - - - - -

_____

Dictation

_____
- - - - - - - - -
_____
- - - - - - - - -
_____
- - - - - - - - -
_____

_____
- - - - - - - - -
_____
- - - - - - - - -
_____
- - - - - - - - -
_____

Directions: Unscramble the letters to correctly name the picture. Write the word on the line.

Phonics • *Skills Practice 1*

Sounds and Spellings

th

Practice

_____   _____   _____

Directions: Practice writing *th* in the space provided. At the bottom, name each picture. Write *th* if you hear the /th/ sound in the word.

Apply

math thin thread
thick cloth

1.

2.

3. $$\begin{array}{r} 1 \\ +2 \\ \hline 3 \end{array} \qquad \begin{array}{r} 3 \\ +1 \\ \hline 4 \end{array}$$

_____

- - - - - - - - - - - -

_____

4.

5.

_____

- - - - - - - - - - - -

_____

Directions: Name each picture. Write the word that names the picture.

Phonics • *Skills Practice 1*

Sounds and Spellings

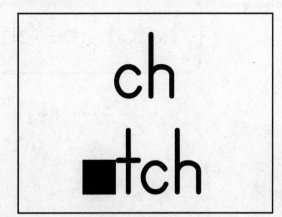

ch _

■tch _ _ _ _ _ _ _ _ _ _ _ _ _ _ _ _ _ _ _

Practice

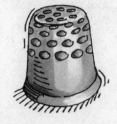

___ ___ ___ ___

_ _ _ _ _ _ _ _

___ ___ ___ ___

Directions: Practice writing *ch* and ■*tch* in the spaces provided. Use a green crayon to draw the box in the ■*tch* spelling. At the bottom, name the picture. Write *ch* if you hear the /ch/ sound at the beginning of the word.

Apply

hatch   bench   chip

1.

_____

- - - - - - - - -

_____

2.

_____

- - - - - - - - -

_____

3.

_____

- - - - - - - - -

_____

Dictation

_____   _____

- - - - - - - - -   - - - - - - - - -

_____   _____

- - - - - - - - -   - - - - - - - - -

_____   _____

- - - - - - - - -   - - - - - - - - -

_____   _____

Directions: Name each picture. Write the word that names the picture.

Telling Sentences

Focus

Rule	Example
A sentence tells a thought. A **telling sentence** begins with a capital letter and ends with a period (.).	Birds make nests.

Practice

1. A big fish swims in the ocean.

2. Is it napping?

3. There is a starfish on the hill.

4. It sits still on the sand.

Directions: Listen to each sentence. Circle the telling sentences.

Apply

5. tom has frogs

6. he is at the pond

7. he dumps the frogs into a glass box

8. the frogs sit

Directions: Read each sentence. Write the sentences correctly on the lines. Use a capital letter and a period.

Sounds and Spellings Review

bread

chest

ship

stretch

watch

chimp

head

shack

month

bench

Directions: Read the words. Then connect each word to its picture.

Sounds and Spellings Review

chipmunk up The nut. the picked

_____

- - - - - - - - - - - - - - - - -

_____

- - - - - - - - - - - - - - - - -

_____

- - - - - - - - - - - - - - - - -

_____

Dictation

_____   _____

- - - - - - - -   - - - - - - - -

_____   _____

- - - - - - - -   - - - - - - - -

_____   _____

- - - - - - - -   - - - - - - - -

_____   _____

Directions: Look at the picture. Unscramble the words to make a sentence. Write the sentence correctly on the lines.

Sounds and Spellings

| or |
| ore |

or

ore

Practice

_____ _____ _____

_____ _____ _____

Directions: Practice writing *or* and *ore* on the spaces provided. At the bottom, name each picture.
Write *or* if you hear the /or/ sound in the word.

Apply

cord	stork	horn	corn

1. The _____ blasted when the ship left the dock.

2. The class saw a _____ _____ on a nest.

3. The boy led the horse with a _____ _____.

4. Ann had _____ _____ on the cob.

Directions: Write the word from the box that correctly completes each sentence. Listen as the teacher reads the sentence.

Phonics • *Skills Practice 1*

Describe a Person

Think

Audience: Who will read your description?

_____

- -

_____

- -

_____

- -

_____

Purpose: What do you want your description to do?

_____

- -

_____

- -

_____

- -

_____

Prewriting

Use the cluster web to organize descriptive words or phrases about your topic.

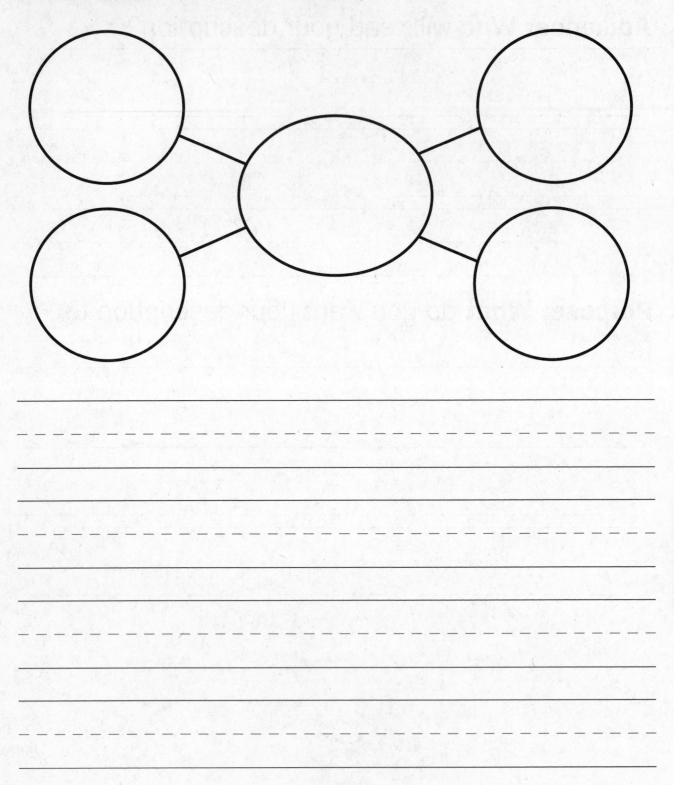

_____

- -

_____

_____

- -

_____

_____

- -

_____

Sounds and Spellings

ar

_ar_

Practice

1.

_____

- - - - - - - - - - - -

_____

2.

_____

- - - - - - - - - - - -

_____

Directions: Practice writing _ar_ in the space provided. At the bottom, name the pictures. Write _ar_ if you hear the /ar/ sound in the word.

Apply

3.

_____

- - - - - - - - - - -

_____

r s a t

4.

_____

- - - - - - - - - - -

_____

r m a

5.

_____

- - - - - - - - - - -

_____

a c d r

6.

_____

- - - - - - - - - - -

_____

e r d g n a

7.

_____

- - - - - - - - - - -

_____

r b n a

8.

_____

- - - - - - - - - - -

_____

a k p r

Directions: Name each picture. Unscramble the letters and write the word correctly on the line.

Sounds and Spellings

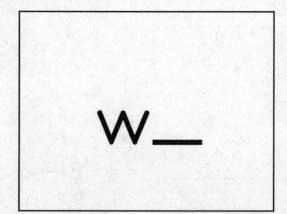

W_

W_

Practice

1. wind _____

2. wax _____

3. wig _____

4. well _____

Directions: Practice writing *w_* and *W_* in the spaces provided. Say each word and write it correctly on the line.

Apply

5.

_____

_____

6.

_____

_____

7.

_____

_____

8.

_____

_____

9.

_____

_____

10.

_____

_____

Dictation

_____ _____

_____ _____

_____ _____

_____ _____

_____ _____

Directions: Say the name of each picture. Write a w after the words that begin with the /w/ sound.

Phonics • *Skills Practice 1*

Sounds and Spellings

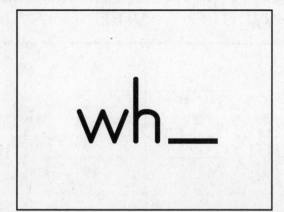
wh_

wh_ -

Practice

_____

- - - - - - - - -

_____

_____

- - - - - - - - -

_____

Directions: Practice writing *wh_* in the space provided. Name each picture. Write *wh_* if you hear the /w/ sound at the beginning of the word.

Apply

whiz	what	whip	whack	when

1. Did Ruth _____ the eggs?

2. Did you _____ the ball with a bat?

3. _____ will he get a dog?

4. Bill is a _____ at math.

5. _____ did Liz have for lunch?

Directions: Write the word that completes each sentence in the spaces provided.

Forming Questions

Focus

Rule	Example
A sentence that asks is called a **question**. A question begins with a capital letter and ends with a question mark (**?**).	**M**ay we go to the park**?**

Practice

It is dark. Can we see the stars? We can sit on the back porch. Are there a lot of stars? Will we see a comet? What is a comet? It runs among the stars. Can you see a comet?

Directions: Listen to each sentence. Circle the sentences that ask questions.

Apply

1. where is the pig

_____

- - - - - - - - - - - - - -

_____

2. when did it get out of the pen

_____

- - - - - - - - - - - - - -

_____

- - - - - - - - - - - - - -

_____

3. what is in the barn

_____

- - - - - - - - - - - - - -

_____

4. who will look in the corn bin

_____

- - - - - - - - - - - - - -

_____

Directions: Rewrite the sentences correctly on the lines. Use a capital letter and a question mark.

Grammar, Usage, and Mechanics • *Skills Practice 1*

Sounds and Spellings Review

or	ore	ar	w	wh

1.

h _____ se

2.

st _____

3.

f _____ mer

4.

_____ ale

5.

_____ ind

6.

g _____ den

Directions: Look at each picture. Insert the missing spelling for each word. Use the spellings in the box to help you.

Sounds and Spellings Review

starfish   whale

7. A _____ is in the sand.

8. A turtle swims behind a _____.

Dictation

Phonics • *Skills Practice 1*

Sounds and Spellings

er ir

er

ir

Practice

fern	wish	send	third

1. _____   2. _____

Directions: Practice writing the letters that make the /er/ sound in the spaces provided. Say each word. Write the words with the /er/ sound on the lines.

Apply

| under | girl | bird | winter |

3.

_____

- - - - - - - - - - - - -

_____

4.

_____

- - - - - - - - - - - - -

_____

5.

_____

- - - - - - - - - - - - -

_____

6.

_____

- - - - - - - - - - - - -

_____

Dictation

_____

- - - - - - - - - - - - -

_____

- - - - - - - - - - - - -

_____

- - - - - - - - - - - - -

_____

- - - - - - - - - - - - -

_____

- - - - - - - - - - - - -

Directions: Write the word on the line that names the picture.

Revising
Use this checklist to make your description better.

☐ Did you use your web to help you organize descriptive words for your writing?

☐ Did you use telling sentences to write details about your topic?

☐ Do the details in your description help the reader picture the person?

Editing
Use this checklist to help make corrections to your description.

☐ Did you begin the first word of each sentence with a capital letter?

☐ Did you write in complete sentences?

☐ Are all the words spelled correctly?

Publishing

Use this checklist to get your description ready to share.

☐ Copy your description onto a clean sheet of paper.

☐ Add an illustration to your writing.

Sounds and Spellings

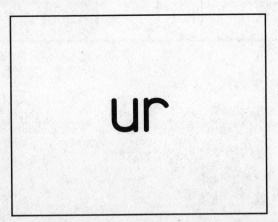

ur

ur

Practice

| curl | cub | curb | hurt | him |

1. _____

2. _____

3. _____

Directions: Practice writing the letters *ur* on the line. Say each word. Write the words with the /er/ sound on the lines.

Apply

| surf | hurt | burn | turn | fur |

4.

_____
- - - - - - - - - - - - - - - -
_____

5.

_____
- - - - - - - - - - - - - - - -
_____

6.

_____
- - - - - - - - - - - - - - - -
_____

7.

_____
- - - - - - - - - - - - - - - -
_____

8.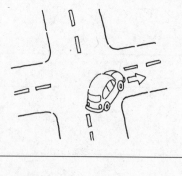

_____
- - - - - - - - - - - - - - - -
_____

Directions: Write the word on the line that names the picture.

Phonics • *Skills Practice 1*

Sounds and Spellings

/er/ as in **ear**ly

Practice

earth   pearl   search   early

1.

_____

- - - - - - - - - - - - - - -

_____

2.

_____

- - - - - - - - - - - - - - -

_____

3.

_____

- - - - - - - - - - - - - - -

_____

4.

_____

- - - - - - - - - - - - - - -

_____

Directions: Write the word that correctly names each picture.

Apply

earns   search   learn   heard

5. Earl likes to _____ about the world.

6. Earl likes to _____ the map for new places.

7. Earl has _____ about far-off lands.

8. Earl _____ money so he can take a fun trip.

Directions: Write the word on the line that correctly completes each sentence.

Sounds and Spellings

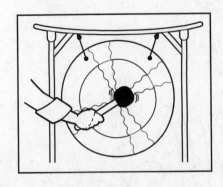

■ng

Practice

ring	band	rock	stung
help	cling	hang	land

1. _____

2. _____

3. _____

4. _____

Directions: Practice writing ■ng in the space provided. Next read the words in the box. Write the
words that end with the /ng/ sound on the lines.

Apply

swing	clang

5.

_____

- - - - - - - - - - - -

_____

6.

_____

- - - - - - - - - - - -

_____

Dictation

_____

- - - - - - - - - - - - - - - - -

_____

- - - - - - - - - - - - - - - - -

_____

- - - - - - - - - - - - - - - - -

_____

_____

- - - - - - - - - - - - - - - - -

_____

- - - - - - - - - - - - - - - - -

_____

- - - - - - - - - - - - - - - - -

_____

Directions: Read the word in the box. Write the word that names each picture on the lines.

Exclamatory Sentences
Focus

> **Rule**
> An **exclamatory sentence** is a sentence that has strong feeling. It starts with a capital letter and ends with an exclamation point (**!**).
>
> **Example**
> **T**he song is great**!**

Practice

1. What is her name?

2. I got skates!

3. Allison helped make this dress.

4. The bug is big!

5. That was fun!

Directions: Read each sentence. Circle the exclamatory sentences.

Apply

6. was there a crash

_____

- -

_____

7. look, it is Tanzer

_____

- -

_____

8. he was taking a nap in the closet

_____

- -

_____

- -

Directions: Read each sentence. Write the sentences correctly on the line.
Use a capital letter to begin the sentence and correct punctuation at the end.

Grammar, Usage, and Mechanics • *Skills Practice 1*

Sounds and Spellings Review

| ir | er | ur | ear |

1. st _____

2. bak _____

3. riv _____

4. l _____ n

5. t _____ n

6. _____ th

7. p _____ l

8. b _____ n

Directions: Choose the correct spelling of the /er/ sound to complete each word.

Sounds and Spellings Review

ring

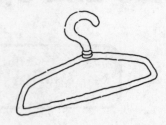

song

prongs

swing

hanger

Directions: Read the words. Then connect each word to its picture.

Phonics • *Skills Practice 1*

Sounds and Spellings

Rule
The schwa sound is similar to /u/. When you write a word with the schwa sound, ask yourself which vowel spelling you should use.

Practice

Directions: Say the word that names the picture. Circle the pictures that have the schwa sound.

Skills Practice 1 • Phonics

Apply

Josh slips in his sandals.

Josh fed his pet a carrot.

Dictation

Directions: Write the sentence that describes the picture.

Writing Instructions

Think

Audience: Who will follow the instructions?

_____
- -
_____
- -
_____

Purpose: What do you want the instructions to do?

_____
- -
_____
- -
_____

Prewriting

Use the organizer below to plan the instructions.

First

Next

Then

Last

Revising
Use this checklist to make the instructions better.

☐ Did you use a map to organize ideas for writing?

☐ Did you write the instructions clearly?

☐ Did you arrange sentences in the correct order?

☐ Did you use verbs and time and order words correctly?

Editing
Use this checklist to check the instructions.

☐ Did you correctly capitalize proper nouns and the pronoun I?

☐ Do sentences begin with capital letters and use correct end marks?

Publishing
Use this checklist to get the instructions ready to share.

☐ Copy the edited instructions onto a clean sheet of paper or into your Writer's Notebook.

☐ Create a picture of each step.

Writing • *Skills Practice 1*

Sounds and Spellings

> **Rule**
> The final schwa plus /l/ sound can be spelled -el, -le, -il, or -al.
> Examples: puzzle, local, tunnel, fossil

el

le

il

al

Practice

1. pencil _____

2. little _____

3. petal _____

4. channel _____

Directions: Practice writing the –le, –el, –il, and –al spellings. Read and write the words with the schwa sound.

Apply

-al	-il	-le	-el

5. app _____

6. trav _____

7. tot _____

8. foss _____

9. met _____

10. shov _____

11. pudd _____

12. nostr _____

Directions: Use one of the spellings of the schwa sound in the box to complete each word.

Sounds and Spellings

■nk

Practice

drink   skunk   blanket

1.

_____
- - - - - - - - - -
_____

2.

_____
- - - - - - - - - -
_____

3.

_____
- - - - - - - - - -
_____

Directions: Practice writing ■nk in the space provided. Use a green crayon to draw the green box in the spelling. At the bottom, name each picture. Write the word that names the picture on the lines.

Apply

_____   _____

- - - - - - - - - - - - - -   - - - - - - - - - - - - - -

_____   _____

- - - - - - - - - - - - - -   - - - - - - - - - - - - - -

_____   _____

Dictation

_____   _____

- - - - - - - - - - - - - -   - - - - - - - - - - - - - -

_____   _____

- - - - - - - - - - - - - -   - - - - - - - - - - - - - -

_____   _____

- - - - - - - - - - - - - -   - - - - - - - - - - - - - -

_____   _____

Directions: Read the word on the bottle. Use the letters on the paper to
write rhyming words on the lines.

Sounds and Spellings

qu_

qu_

Qu_

Practice

1. quiz _____   2. quack _____

3. The quilt has stars.

_____

Directions: Practice writing *qu_* and *Qu_* in the spaces provided. Then write the words and sentence on the lines.

Practice

4. i sh qu s   5. z qu i

_____

- - - - - - - - - - - - -

_____

6. i t qu l   7. qu d i s

_____

- - - - - - - - - - - - -

_____

8. ck i qu   9. l i qu l   10. a ck qu

_____

- - - - - - - - - - - - -

_____

Directions: Unscramble the letters and correctly write the word on the line that names the picture.

Imperative Sentences
Focus

Rule	Example
An **imperative sentence** gives an order, a request, or a demand, or expresses a wish. It starts with a capital letter and ends with a period (.) or an exclamation point (!).	Fill the dog's dish. A car is coming!

Practice

1. This is a fire drill.

2. Line up in the hall.

3. Do not yell!

4. Walk to the yard.

5. The class is safe!

Directions: Read each sentence and circle the imperative sentences.

Apply

6. line up at this mark

_____

- - - - - - - - - - - - - - - - - - - -

_____

7. listen for the horn

_____

- - - - - - - - - - - - - - - - - - - -

_____

8. run for the finish line

_____

- - - - - - - - - - - - - - - - - - - -

_____

Directions: Listen to each sentence. Write the sentence correctly on the line. Begin the sentence with a capital letter and put a period or exclamation point at the end.

Sounds and Spellings Review

| table | snorkel | think | coral | quilt | moccasin |

1.

_____

- - - - - - - - - - - - - - -

_____

2.

_____

- - - - - - - - - - - - - - -

_____

3.

_____

- - - - - - - - - - - - - - -

_____

4.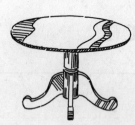

_____

- - - - - - - - - - - - - - -

_____

5.

_____

- - - - - - - - - - - - - - -

_____

6.

_____

- - - - - - - - - - - - - - -

_____

Directions: Write the word that names each picture.

Sounds and Spellings Review

_nk   qu_   -le

kett   ack   tru

Dictation

_____   _____

_____   _____

_____   _____

_____   _____

_____   _____

Directions: Name each picture. Write the letters from the box to complete the words.

Sounds and Spellings

Y_

Practice

y_   Y_

1. yell _____   2. yard _____

3. Do they have yams?

_____

Directions: Practice writing y_ and Y_. Write the words and the sentence in the space provided.

Apply

4.

_____

- - - - - - - - -

_____

5.

_____

- - - - - - - - -

_____

6.

_____

- - - - - - - - -

_____

Dictation

_____

- - - - - - - - -

_____

- - - - - - - - -

_____

- - - - - - - - -

_____

Directions: Say the name of each picture. Write the letter _y_ on the line if the word begins with the sound /y/.

Phonics • *Skills Practice 1*

Writing Instructions
Think
Audience: **Who** will follow the instructions?

Purpose: **What** do you want the instructions to do?

Prewriting
Use the organizer below to plan the instructions.

First

Next

Then

Last

Revising
Use this checklist to make the instructions better.

☐ Did you use a map to organize ideas for writing?

☐ Did you write sentences clearly?

☐ Do all steps have time and order words?

☐ Did you arrange sentences in the correct order?

Editing
Use this checklist to check the instructions.

☐ Do all words have correct spellings?

☐ Did you write in complete sentences?

☐ Do all sentences begin with capital letters and have the correct end marks?

Publishing
Use this checklist to get the instructions ready to share.

☐ Copy the edited instructions onto a clean sheet of paper or into your Writer's Notebook.

☐ Create a picture of each step.

Sounds and Spellings

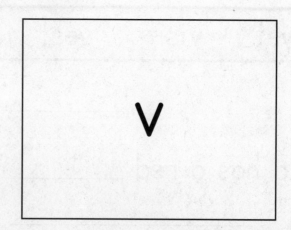

V

Practice

v   V

1. vet _____ 2. van _____

3. Vince is seven.

_____

_____

Directions: Practice writing v and V. Write the words and the sentence in the spaces provided.

Apply

| vet | visit | vest | seven | van |

4. Vic has a red _____.

5. The _____ is parked by the curb.

6. The dog went to the _____.

7. I will turn _____ in March.

8. Kevin will _____ his grandma.

Directions: Read the words in the box. Write a word on the line to complete each sentence.

Phonics • *Skills Practice 1*

Sounds and Spellings

a

a_e

Practice

whale _____   cave _____

April _____   sale _____

Jake will staple the papers.

_____

_____

_____

Directions: Write the words and the sentence on the lines.

Apply

gate   game   brake

I am part of a car.
I make the car stop.
What am I?

_____

- -

_____

Dictation

_____

- -

_____

- -

_____

- -

_____

Directions: Read the riddle. Write the word that answers the riddle.

Sounds and Spellings

a

a_e

Practice

cable _____   late _____

radar _____   plane _____

mate _____   bacon _____

Dave is able to skate.

_____

_____

Directions: Write the words and the sentence on the lines provided.

Apply

| tape | rake | ape | plane |

1.

_____

- - - - - - - - - - - -

_____

2.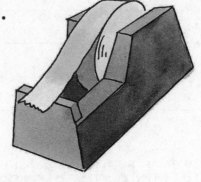

_____

- - - - - - - - - - - -

_____

3.

_____

- - - - - - - - - - - -

_____

4.

_____

- - - - - - - - - - - -

_____

Directions: Write the word that names each picture on the line.

Phonics • *Skills Practice 1*

Determiners

Focus

> Articles are a type of determiners. The words *a, an,* and *the* are special words called **articles**.

Practice

1. This dog is cute.

2. I had a sandwich for lunch.

3. Where did Gene put those books?

4. That water is cold.

5. Can Lisa have an apple?

Directions: Listen to each sentence. Circle the article in each sentence.

Apply

1. Where is _____ library?

_____the these_____

2. Tom needs _____ pencil.

_____an   a_____

3. _____ boats are purple.

_____These This_____

4. Kim wants _____ sweater.

_____those that_____

5. Ben filled _____ glass.

_____the these_____

Directions: Listen to each sentence. Circle the correct determiner and write it on the line.

Sounds and Spellings Review

vase

cake

table

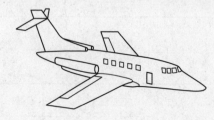

plane

yell

Directions: Read the words. Then connect each word to its picture.

Sounds and Spellings Review

1. We see fish in the _____.   scale   lake

2. Pat is _____ to help.   apple   able

3. Tate ate a _____.   grape   gap

Dictation

_____   _____

_____   _____

_____   _____

_____   _____

_____   _____

Directions: Complete each sentence with the correct word.

Phonics • *Skills Practice 1*

Sounds and Spellings

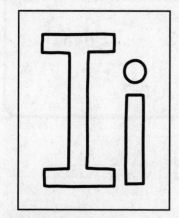 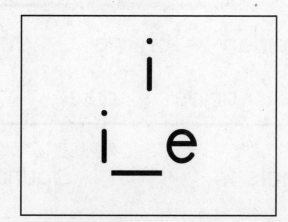

Practice

tiger _____

time _____

pipe _____

title _____

mile _____

ride _____

Did he find a dime?

_____

_____

Directions: Write the words and sentence on the lines.

Apply

child	spider	chime	wife	silent
	lion	bride	quiet	tiger

Animals

_____

_____

_____

Sound Words

_____

_____

_____

People

_____

_____

Directions: Listen as the teacher reads each heading. Write the words on
the lines under the correct heading.

Opinion Statement

Think

Audience: Who will read the writing?

_____

_____

Purpose: What do you want the writing to do?

_____

_____

Prewriting

Complete the web to help get ideas for your opinion statement.

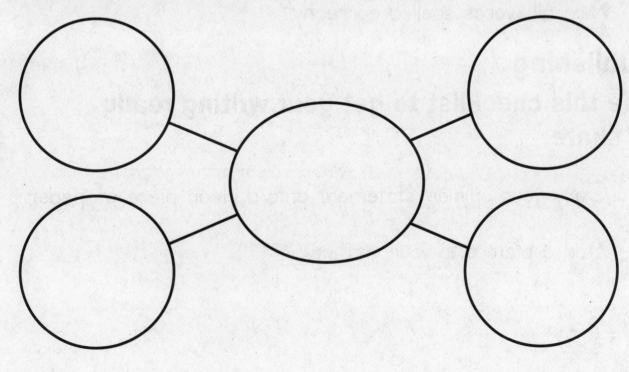

Revising
Use this checklist to revise your opinion statement.

☐ Did you clearly state your opinion?

☐ Does every sentence tell about your opinion?

☐ Did you add descriptive details to your sentences?

Editing/Proofreading
Use this checklist to help correct mistakes.

☐ Did you start the first word of each sentence with a capital letter?

☐ Did you write in complete sentences?

☐ Are all words spelled correctly?

Publishing
Use this checklist to get your writing ready to share.

☐ Copy your opinion statement onto a clean piece of paper.

☐ Add a picture to your writing.

Sounds and Spellings

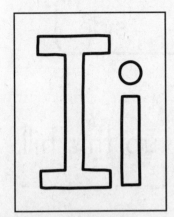   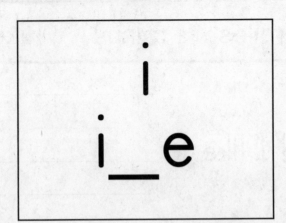

Practice

1. _____ 2. _____ 3. _____

  i n n e   m e i d   e v n i

Directions: Unscramble the letters and write the word that names the picture.

Apply

time	miles	minus	hike	side

4. Mike and I like to _____ up this hill.

5. We can walk five _____.

6. We rest at the _____ of the path.

Dictation

_____   _____

_____   _____

_____   _____

_____   _____

Directions: Read each sentence. Write the word that correctly completes the sentence.

Phonics • *Skills Practice 1*

Sounds and Spellings

ce
ci_

Practice

cent _____   cell _____

circle _____   pace _____

Grace has six cents.

_____

_____

Directions: Write the words and sentence in the spaces provided.

Apply

face   crate   race   candle

picnic   carrot   lace   space

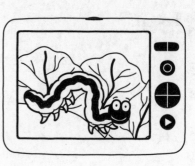

_____   _____

_____   _____

_____   _____

_____   _____

_____   _____

_____   _____

Directions: Write each word under the correct **Sound/Spelling Card** picture
for /s/ or /k/.

188 UNIT 5 • Lesson 1 • Day 3

Phonics • *Skills Practice 1*

Sounds and Spellings

ge
gi_

Practice

gem _____   rage _____

_____

gel _____

I. There is ginger in the jam.

_____

_____

Directions: Write the words and the sentence in the spaces provided.

Apply

_____   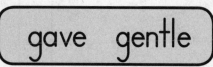 jar   bridge

2. Kate has a _____ of jam.

_____   gave   gentle

3. Tim was _____ with the cat.

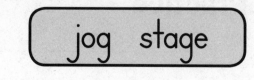 jog   stage

_____

4. We had a skit on the _____.

Dictation

_____   _____

_____   _____

_____   _____

_____   _____

_____   _____

Directions: Complete each sentence with the correct word from the box.
Write the word on the line.

Phonics • *Skills Practice 1*

Capitalization
Focus

Rule	Example
• People's names are proper nouns and start with **capital letters**. The word *I* is always written with a capital letter.	**K**ate **N**elson **I**
• Names of special things and special places are also proper nouns and start with **a capital letter**.	**B**ates **M**anor **G**olden **G**ate **B**ridge

Practice

1. james madison _____

_____

2. the alamo _____

_____

3. the black sea _____

_____

4. mike smith _____

Directions: Rewrite the words using capital letters.

Apply

5. alex and lisa went to a picnic at twin coves park.

_____

_____

_____

6. eric stallman and i tossed the ball.

_____

_____

7. mr. smith made a big lunch.

_____

_____

8. uncle dan paddled on mead lake.

_____

_____

Directions: Listen as the teacher reads each sentence. Circle the words that should start with a capital letter. Then write the words correctly on the lines.

Sounds and Spellings Review

| circus | cage | bridge | palace | pencil | giant |

1.

_____
- - - - - - - - - - - - - - -
_____

2.

_____
- - - - - - - - - - - - - - -
_____

3.

_____
- - - - - - - - - - - - - - -
_____

4.

_____
- - - - - - - - - - - - - - -
_____

5.

_____
- - - - - - - - - - - - - - -
_____

6.

_____
- - - - - - - - - - - - - - -
_____

Directions: Name each picture. Write the correct word on the line.

Sounds and Spellings Review

pile   race   place   gerbils
cage   tile   change   garbage

7. Oh no! The _____ _____

   got out of their _____.

8. I saw them _____ across

   the _____ floor.

9. Are they behind the _____

   can?

10. I see them under the _____

    of socks in the basket.

Directions: Listen as the teacher reads each sentence. Write the word or words that correctly complete each sentence. You will not use all of the words.

Phonics • *Skills Practice 1*

Sounds and Spellings

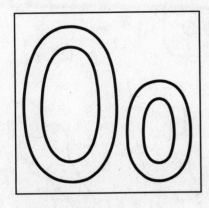

o
o_e

Practice

_____   _____

- - - - - - - - - - - - - - -   - - - - - - - - - - - - - - -

no _____   rode _____

1. The dog hid a bone.

_____

- -

_____

2. I broke the pole.

_____

- -

_____

Directions: Write the words and sentences in the spaces provided.

Apply

rope   bone   stone

3.

4.

5.
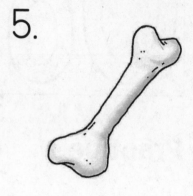

_____

- - - - - - - - - - - - -

_____

_____

- - - - - - - - - - - - -

_____

_____

- - - - - - - - - - - - -

_____

Dictation

_____

- - - - - - - - - - - - -

_____

- - - - - - - - - - - - -

_____

- - - - - - - - - - - - -

_____

Directions: Write the word that names each picture.

UNIT 5 • Lesson 2 • Day 1

Phonics • *Skills Practice 1*

Copyright © McGraw-Hill Education

Persuasive Poster
Think
Audience: Who will read your persuasive poster?

_____

- -

_____

_____

- -

_____

Purpose: What do you want your persuasive
poster to do?

_____

- -

_____

_____

- -

_____

Prewriting
Brainstorm places in your community.

- - - - - - - - - - - - - -	- - - - - - - - - - - - - -
_____	_____
- - - - - - - - - - - - - -	- - - - - - - - - - - - - -
_____	_____
- - - - - - - - - - - - - -	- - - - - - - - - - - - - -
_____	_____

Prewriting

Complete the web to help get ideas for your poster.

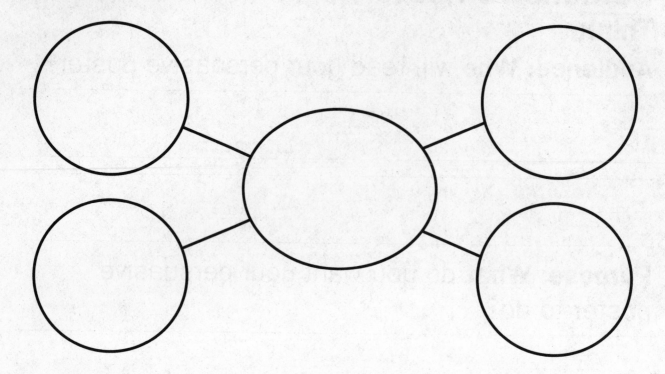

Drafting

Use the space below to draft your poster.

Sounds and Spellings Review

| home   cones   tornado   nose   robe   potato |

1.

_____

- - - - - - - - - - - - - - - - -

_____

2.

_____

- - - - - - - - - - - - - - - - -

_____

3.

_____

- - - - - - - - - - - - - - - - -

_____

4.

_____

- - - - - - - - - - - - - - - - -

_____

5.

_____

- - - - - - - - - - - - - - - - -

_____

6.

_____

- - - - - - - - - - - - - - - - -

_____

Directions: Name each picture. Write the correct word on the line.

Sounds and Spellings Review

globe	awoke	holes	alone

7. Margo _____
late this morning.

8. Can you find Mexico

_____

on the _____?

9. The pup nibbles _____

in the sock.

10. The kitten was

_____

_____.

Directions: Look at the picture. Write the word that correctly completes each sentence.

Phonics • *Skills Practice 1*

Sounds and Spellings

Practice

use _____

_____

music _____

cute _____

I. The mule likes ice cubes.

_____

_____

_____

Directions: Write the words and sentence in the spaces provided.

Apply

2. The mule is cute.

The mule licks an ice cube.

_____

- -

_____

Dictation

_____   _____

- - - - - - - - - - - - - -   - - - - - - - - - - - - - -

_____   _____

- - - - - - - - - - - - - -   - - - - - - - - - - - - - -

_____   _____

- - - - - - - - - - - - - -   - - - - - - - - - - - - - -

_____   _____

- - - - - - - - - - - - - -   - - - - - - - - - - - - - -

_____   _____

Directions: Write the sentence described by the picture.

Sounds and Spellings Review

cute   use

m   f

_____   _____

1. The small kitten is _____.

cub   cute

2. Gus picked a _____ apple.

hug   huge

Directions: Read each word. Use the letter under the word to write a word that rhymes with it. Then write the word that completes each sentence.

Sounds and Spellings Review

bugle   menu   mule

3. I am an instrument.

I make music.

What am I?

_____

- - - - - - - - - - - - -

_____

4. A barn is my home.

I am an animal.

What am I?

_____

- - - - - - - - - - - - -

_____

5. I am a list.

I can have the cost of a sandwich.

What am I?

_____

- - - - - - - - - - - - -

_____

Directions: Read each riddle. Write the correct word on the line.

Phonics • *Skills Practice 1*

Capitalization and Commas

Focus

Rule	Examples
• Days and months begin with **capital letters**.	**M**onday **A**pril
• Use **commas** between the day, date, and year.	**M**onday, January 13, 1980

Practice

_____

1. sunday _____

_____

2. march _____

_____

3. october 15 2010 _____

_____

4. april 25 2009 _____

Directions: Listen. Write the day, month, or date correctly on the lines.

Apply

5. Logan has soccer practice every friday.

_____

- -

_____

6. Classes started on september 1 2009.

_____

- -

_____

7. The Smith family will visit Gram on october 5 2016.

_____

- -

_____

8. Dotty will go to the concert on thursday.

_____

- -

_____

Directions: Read each sentence. Circle the word in each sentence that should start with a capital letter. Then write the day of the week or the date correctly on the lines

Grammar, Usage, and Mechanics • *Skills Practice 1*

Sounds and Spellings Review

bone

mule

vine

cage

note

music

Directions: Read the words. Then connect each word to its picture.

Sounds and Spellings Review

holes the Moles yard. dig in

_____

- -

_____

- -

_____

Dictation

_____   _____

- - - - - - - - - - - - - - -   - - - - - - - - - - - - - - -

_____   _____

- - - - - - - - - - - - - - -   - - - - - - - - - - - - - - -

_____   _____

- - - - - - - - - - - - - - -   - - - - - - - - - - - - - - -

_____   _____

- - - - - - - - - - - - - - -   - - - - - - - - - - - - - - -

_____   _____

Directions: Look at the picture. Unscramble the words to make a sentence.
Write the sentence correctly on the line.

Phonics • *Skills Practice 1*

Sounds and Spellings

e

e_e

Practice

be _____   Gene _____

we _____   these _____

me _____

1. Steve will be here.

_____

_____

_____

Directions: Write the words and sentence in the spaces provided.

Apply

zebra   cedar

_____

2. A _____ is a black

and white animal.

car   fever

_____

3. Pete has a _____.

Dictation

_____   _____

_____   _____

_____   _____

_____   _____

_____   _____

_____   _____

Directions: Look at each picture. Complete the sentence with the
correct word.

Persuasive Poster
Revising

Use the space below to revise your poster.

Revising
Use this checklist to make your poster better.

☐ Does your poster help readers to think or feel a certain way?

☐ Did you add sensory details to the picture and the text?

Editing/Proofreading
Use this checklist to help correct mistakes.

☐ Did you start the first word of each sentence with a capital letter?

☐ Did you use correct end marks?

☐ Are all words spelled correctly?

Publishing
Use this checklist to get your persuasive poster ready to share.

☐ Does your poster have a picture and text?

☐ Is your poster bright and colorful?

Sounds and Spellings Review

me	She	be	meters	athlete

1. Steve is an _____.

2. Leta gave the ball to _____.

3. The game will _____ at ten.

4. _____ is Pete's sister.

5. Eve can run ten _____.

Directions: Write the word that completes each sentence.

Sounds and Spellings Review

eve   Topic of a story

theme   A man's name

these   All of something

extreme   The evening before

trapeze   Not he

Steven   A circus act

she   Not those

complete   Too much

Directions: Read the words. Then connect each word to its definition.

Phonics • *Skills Practice 1*

Sounds and Spellings

ee

Practice

peek _____   cheek _____

feel _____   meet _____

I. The queen has a green dress.

_____

_____

_____

_____

Directions: Write the words and the sentence in the spaces provided.

Apply

2.

p e s e l

_____

- - - - - - - - -

3.

f d e e

_____

- - - - - - - - -

4.

b e s e

_____

- - - - - - - - -

5.

e t e r

_____

- - - - - - - - -

Dictation

_____
- - - - - - - - -
_____
- - - - - - - - -
_____
- - - - - - - - -
_____

Directions: Look at each picture. Unscramble the letters and write the word
that correctly names the picture.

Phonics • *Skills Practice 1*

Sounds and Spellings

ea

Practice

beak _____

clean _____

treat _____

weak _____

I. Can she teach me to read?

_____

_____

_____

Directions: Write the words and the sentence in the spaces provided.

Apply

2. Jean reaches down to feel the cat.
   Jean reaches down on her ear.

_____

- - - - - - - - - - - - - - - - -

_____

- - - - - - - - - - - - - - - - -

_____

3. Peter sang a song.
   Peter eats his peas.

_____

- - - - - - - - - - - - - - - - -

_____

- - - - - - - - - - - - - - - - -

_____

Directions: Write the sentence that tells about each picture.

Phonics • *Skills Practice 1*

Using Commas and Plural Nouns

Focus

> **Rules**
> - To form the plural of a common noun ending in *y*, change the **y to i**, then add **es**.
> - Commas are used to separate items in a series.
>
> **Examples**
> cit**y**   cit**ies**
> pupp**y**   puppi**es**
>
> We use pencils, paper, and crayons at school.

Practice

1.  kitty _____

2.  guppy _____

3.  bunny _____

Directions: Read each word next to its picture. Write the plural form of the word on the line.

Apply

4. Glenn paid for the book with penny nickel and dime.

_____

- - - - - - - - - - - - - - - - - - - -

_____

- - - - - - - - - - - - - - - - - - - -

_____

5. Mom packed enough grape cherry and banana for everyone.

_____

- - - - - - - - - - - - - - - - - - - -

_____

- - - - - - - - - - - - - - - - - - - -

_____

Directions: Listen to each sentence. Rewrite the sentences on the lines, changing the nouns from singular to plural and adding commas in the appropriate places.

Grammar, Usage, and Mechanics • *Skills Practice 1*

Sounds and Spellings Review

| wheel beads meter sweep concrete read |

1.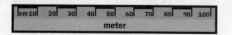

2.

3.

_____

4.

5.

6.

_____

Directions: Write the word that names each picture.

Sounds and Spellings Review

7. You _____ with your ear.

here   hear

8. Dean has his feet in the
_____
_____.

creak   creek

Dictation

_____   _____

_____   _____

_____   _____

_____

Directions: Look at the pictures and complete each sentence with the
correct word.

Phonics • *Skills Practice 1*

Sounds and Spellings

 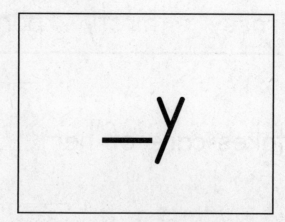

Practice

copy _____   lady _____

body _____   easy _____

1. The tiny baby is sleepy.

_____

_____

_____

_____

Directions: Write the words and the sentence in the spaces provided.

Apply

grassy thirsty pony dirty

2. Sally takes care of her _____.

3. She lets him run in a _____ yard.

4. She cleans him when he is _____.

5. Sally brings him
water when he is _____.

Directions: Write the word that completes each sentence.

Responding to Literature
Think

Audience: Who will read the writing?

_____

- -

_____

Purpose: What do you want the writing to do?

_____

- -

_____

Prewriting

Use the web to think of ideas for the writing.

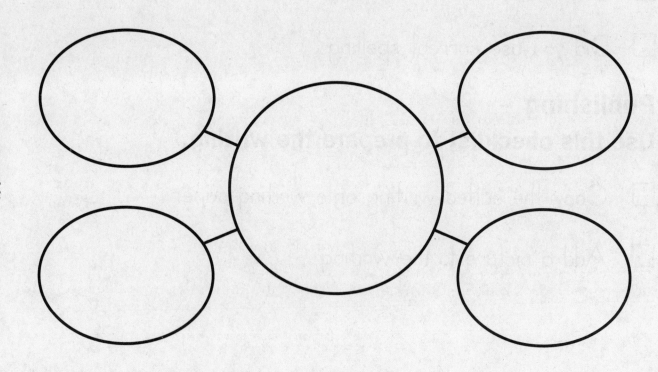

Revising
Use this checklist to make the writing better.

☐ Did the web help you think of ideas for the writing?

☐ Is the writing on topic?

☐ Did you use proofreading marks to add and delete words that make the writing clearer?

Editing
Use this checklist to help correct the writing.

☐ Did you use a capital letter with the name of a person, a proper noun, or the pronoun I?

☐ Did you use the correct end mark with every sentence?

☐ Did you use correct spelling?

Publishing
Use this checklist to prepare the writing.

☐ Copy the edited writing onto writing paper.

☐ Add a picture to the writing.

Sounds and Spellings

 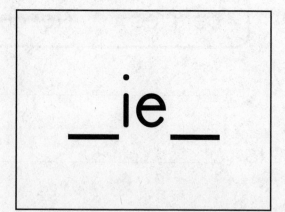

Practice

brief _____   yield _____

field _____   chief _____

1. Annie reads scary stories.

_____

_____

_____

Directions: Write the words and sentence in the spaces provided.

Apply

berries	fierce

2. The lion is _____.

3. We picked _____.

Dictation

_____ _____

_____ _____

_____ _____

_____ _____

Directions: Look at the picture. Write the word that correctly completes the sentence.

Phonics • *Skills Practice 1*

Sounds and Spellings

Practice

_____   _____

key _____   honey _____

1. Ashley likes hockey.

_____

- -

_____

2. Do you need money?

_____

- -

_____

Directions: Write the words and the sentences in the spaces provided.

Apply

3.

y t u e k r

_____

- - - - - - - - - - - - - - - -

_____

4.

e y j r e s

_____

- - - - - - - - - - - - - - - -

_____

Dictation

_____

- - - - - - - - - - - - - - - -

_____

- - - - - - - - - - - - - - - -

_____

- - - - - - - - - - - - - - - -

_____

Directions: Unscramble the letters and write the word that names the picture.

Phonics • *Skills Practice 1*

1.

y c h e m i n

_____

- - - - - - - - -

_____

2.

s n p i e o

_____

- - - - - - - - -

_____

3.

u k e y t r

_____

- - - - - - - - -

_____

4.

t c y i

_____

- - - - - - - - -

_____

5.

y n u b n

_____

- - - - - - - - -

_____

6.

e r s b i e r

_____

- - - - - - - - -

_____

Directions: Unscramble the letters and write the word that names the picture.

Sounds and Spellings Review

thirty	babies	valley

7.

_____

- - - - - - - - - - - - -

_____

8.

_____

- - - - - - - - - - - - -

_____

9.

_____

- - - - - - - - - - - - -

_____

money	windy	ladies

10.

_____

- - - - - - - - - - - - -

_____

11.

_____

- - - - - - - - - - - - -

_____

12.

_____

- - - - - - - - - - - - -

_____

Directions: Write the word that goes with each picture.

Phonics • *Skills Practice 1*

Simple Sentences and Subject-Verb Agreement
Focus

Rules	Examples
• Sentences begin with capital letters, leave space between words, and end with correct punctuation.	The dog wags his tail.
• Complete sentences must always have a subject and a verb. A subject and verb must agree in number.	The dogs wag their tails.

Practice

1. Three girls jump rope together.

2. Andre run to catch the ball.

3. They laugh on the playground.

4. Marsha play hopscotch by herself.

Directions: Listen to the sentences. Circle the sentences with correct subject-verb agreement.
Draw a line through the sentences with incorrect subject-verb agreement.

Apply

5. sampaddlehercanoe

_____

- - - - - - - - - - - - - - - - - - - -

_____

- - - - - - - - - - - - - - - - - - - -

_____

- - - - - - - - - - - - - - - - - - - -

_____

6. thekidslistenstotheirteacher

_____

- - - - - - - - - - - - - - - - - - - -

_____

- - - - - - - - - - - - - - - - - - - -

_____

- - - - - - - - - - - - - - - - - - - -

_____

Directions: Listen to each sentence. Rewrite each sentence using correct capitalization, spacing and punctuation. Change the verb in each sentence so it agrees with the subject.

Sounds and Spellings Review

sandy	seashell

_____

1. Pete runs on the _____
   beach.

2. He sees a _____.

hockey	shriek

_____

3. Charlie is on a _____
   team.

4. The fans _____ when
   Charlie scores!

Directions: Write the correct word to complete each sentence.

Sounds and Spellings Review

5. The bird is near the chimney.

   The bird is in a leafy tree.

_____

- -

_____

- -

_____

Dictation

_____   _____

- - - - - - - - - - - - - -   - - - - - - - - - - - - - -

_____   _____

_____   _____

- - - - - - - - - - - - - -   - - - - - - - - - - - - - -

_____   _____

Directions: Write the sentence that tells about the picture.

Sounds and Spellings

cy

Practice

_____   _____

icy _____   fancy _____

1. Tracy eats spicy things.

_____

_____

2. Percy likes to read.

_____

_____

Directions: Write the words and the sentences in the spaces provided.

Apply

3. _____ hears the music.

4. _____ rides his bike.

5. Nancy sees a _____ shirt.

Directions: Look at the pictures. Complete each sentence with the correct word from the box.

Phonics • *Skills Practice 1*

Writing a Summary
Think
Audience: Who will read your summary?

_____

- -

_____

Purpose: What do you want your summary to do?

_____

- -

_____

Prewriting

Plan your summary using the list graphic organizer below.

_____

Title -

_____

1. _____

- -

_____

2. _____

- -

_____

3. _____

- -

_____

4. _____

_____

Revising

Use this checklist to make the response better.

☐ Did you include the most important ideas?

☐ Did you add or delete words, phrases, or sentences to make the writing clearer?

☐ Did you write the title and author at the top of the paper?

☐ Did you write your ideas in the same order as the selection?

Editing

Use this checklist to check the response.

☐ Did you begin each Proper Noun with a capital letter?

☐ Did you spell all words correctly?

☐ Did you write complete sentences?

Publishing

Use this checklist to get your response ready to share.

☐ Copy the response onto writing paper.

Sounds and Spellings Review

dance

seal

pencil

dress

celery

stars

Directions: Read the words. Then draw a line to connect each word to its picture.

Sounds and Spellings Review

cereal	sleepy	circle

1.

2.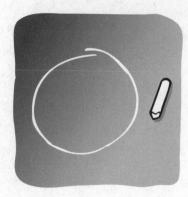

3.

_____   _____   _____

- - - - - - - - - - - -   - - - - - - - - - - - -   - - - - - - - - - - - -

_____   _____   _____

Dictation

_____   _____

- - - - - - - - - - - -   - - - - - - - - - - - -

_____   _____

_____   _____

- - - - - - - - - - - -   - - - - - - - - - - - -

_____   _____

_____   _____

- - - - - - - - - - - -   - - - - - - - - - - - -

Directions: Write the word that names each picture.

Sounds and Spellings

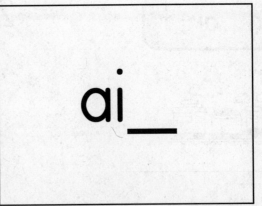

Practice

rain _____   chain _____

maid _____   sail _____

Gail waits at the main gate.

_____

_____

_____

_____

Directions: Write the words and the sentence in the spaces provided.

Apply

1. 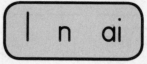 r n ai t

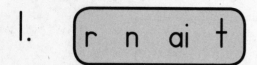

_____
- - - - - - - - - - - -
_____

2. l n ai

_____
- - - - - - - - - - - -
_____

3. l ai t

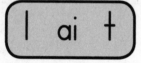

_____
- - - - - - - - - - - -
_____

4. n ai s l

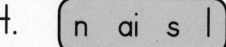

_____
- - - - - - - - - - - -
_____

5. n p ai t

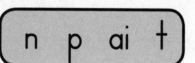

_____
- - - - - - - - - - - -
_____

6. ai l p

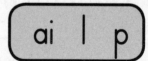

_____
- - - - - - - - - - - -
_____

Directions: Look at each picture. Unscramble the letters and write the word that names the picture.

Phonics • *Skills Practice 1*

Sounds and Spellings

 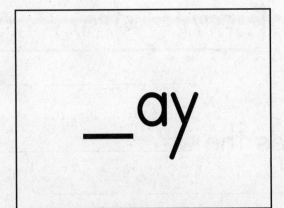

Practice

day _____   play _____

ray _____   stay _____

Directions: Write each word in the space provided. Then place
an X on the picture if it contains the /ā/ sound.

Apply

bay   stray   gray

1. Jay feeds the _____ cat.

2. It is a _____ and rainy day.

3. Ships sail in the _____.

Dictation

_____   _____

_____   _____

_____   _____

_____

Directions: Write a word from the box to complete each sentence.

Writing Sentences
Focus

Rule	Example
Telling sentences end with a period. **(.)** Asking sentences end with a question mark. **(?)** Strong feeling sentences end with an exclamation point. **(!)**	Frogs can jump high. How far can frogs jump? Wow, that frog jumped high!

Practice

1. Was that a skunk?

2. I like to hear music.

3. Sit with me.

4. Tell me a funny story.

5. She is so nice!

6. Is the mail carrier here yet?

Directions: Read each sentence. Circle the imperative sentences (an order, request, or wish) and underline the asking sentences.

Apply

1. Write a strong feeling sentence.

_____

- -

_____

- -

_____

2. Write a telling sentence.

_____

- -

_____

- -

_____

Directions: Look at the picture. Write sentences based on the picture.

Grammar, Usage, and Mechanics • *Skills Practice 1*

Sounds and Spellings Review

quail

day

snail

trail

way

_____

1. It is a sunny _____.

_____

2. The _____ go for a walk.

_____

3. They walk on a _____ to the lake.

_____

4. Mother leads the _____.

_____

5. A baby stops to look at a _____.

Directions: Look at the picture. Complete each sentence with the correct word from the box.

Sounds and Spellings Review

train tray nails paint chain spray

_____
- - - - - - - - -
_____

_____
- - - - - - - - -
_____

Directions: Write the word that names each picture.

250 UNIT 6 • Lesson 2 • Day 5

Phonics • *Skills Practice 1*

Sounds and Spellings

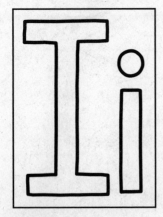

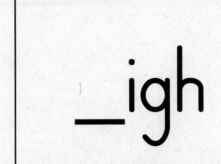

Practice

sigh _____

tight _____

thigh _____

might _____

1. Turn right at the light.

_____

- - - - - - - - - - - - - - - -

_____

- - - - - - - - - - - - - - - -

_____

Directions: Write the words and the sentence in the spaces provided.

Apply

2. fright

3. night

4. bright

Dictation

_____ _____

- - - - - - - - - - - - - - - -   - - - - - - - - - - - - - - - -

_____ _____

- - - - - - - - - - - - - - - -   - - - - - - - - - - - - - - - -

_____ _____

- - - - - - - - - - - - - - - -   - - - - - - - - - - - - - - - -

_____ _____

Directions: Read the words. Then draw a line to connect each word to its picture.

Responding to Literature
Think

Audience: Who will read your response?

_____

- -

_____

Purpose: What do you want your response to do?

_____

- -

_____

Prewriting
Use the sequence map to plan your response.

First

Next

Then

Last

Revising
Use this checklist to make the response better.

☐ Did you stay on topic and include only the most important ideas?

☐ Did you use descriptive, or sensory details?

☐ Did you add or delete words, phrases, or sentences to make the writing clearer?

☐ Did you write the title and author at the top of the paper?

Editing
Use this checklist to check the response.

☐ Did you capitalize the beginning of every sentence, the title, and the author's name?

☐ Did you use correct punctuation at the end of every sentence?

☐ Did you spell all words correctly?

Publishing
Use this checklist to prepare the response to share.

☐ Copy the response onto writing paper.

☐ Make an illustration to go with the response.

Sounds and Spellings

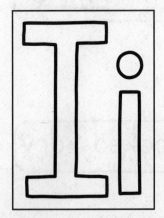

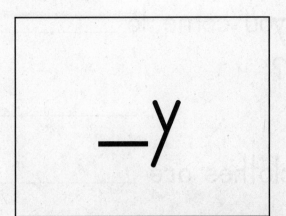

Practice

my _____

sly _____

try _____

cry _____

gate   apply   bend   spy

1. _____

2. _____

Directions: Write the words in the spaces provided. Then, say each word in the box. Write the words with the /ī/ sound.

Apply

3. Can you come to _____ party? `my  mine`

4. The clothes are _____. `baked  dry`

5. Do you see the plane _____ in the _____? `skip  sky`

6. The baby might _____. `cry  shop`

7. _____ don't you go to sleep? `Why  If`

8. Emma is not _____ at home. `short  shy`

Directions: Write the correct word from the box to complete each sentence.

Sounds and Spellings

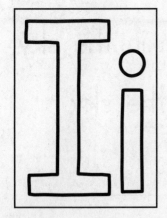

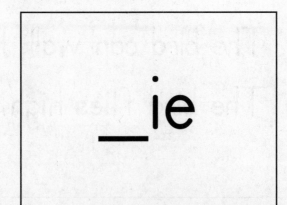

Practice

lie _____ fried _____

pie _____ cried _____

I. Mike tries to swim.

_____

_____

Directions: Write the words and the sentence in the spaces provided.

Apply

2. The bird can walk high in the sky.
   The bird flies high in the sky.

_____

- - - - - - - - - - - - - - - - - - - -

_____

- - - - - - - - - - - - - - - - - - - -

_____

Dictation

_____   _____

- - - - - - - - - - - - - -   - - - - - - - - - - - - - -

_____   _____

- - - - - - - - - - - - - -   - - - - - - - - - - - - - -

_____   _____

- - - - - - - - - - - - - -   - - - - - - - - - - - - - -

_____   _____

Directions: Write the sentence that describes the picture.

Phonics • *Skills Practice 1*